Lunch
With
Lucille

An inspiring story of how a four-diamond
brooch led a woman to discover she is her
best asset — at any age

Annarose Ingarra-Milch

ISBN: 978-0-9854397-0-5

Editor in Chief: Cecile E. Kandl Ph.D
Editor: Lisa McGowan, M.A.

This book was set in Bookman Old Style
Cover Design: Debra Deysher

Coach: Catherine Preziosi

Printed in the United States of America

From the Desk of Annarose

Welcome!

My guess is if you are reading this you are probably like me, one of the over 35 million women who has already celebrated her 40th birthday. When you look in the mirror or stop and think about your age, you probably look somewhat different, you may even act quite differently, and yet you don't feel that much different than you used to feel.

But you are still wondering, how did I get here? It happened so quickly. And now what?

Before any more time passes, you need to read this book. *Lunch with Lucille* is an inspirational dialogue that will both move you and guide you to embrace your best asset—you!

Get ready. It's time to have . . .

Lunch With *Lucille*

Annarose

P. S. Please consider this my personal invitation to eavesdrop on a life changing conversation. Your table is waiting. Come, have Lunch with Lucille.

Buon Appetito!

Annarose Ingarra-Milch

HERE WE GO

I am having another day of feeling overwhelmed and undervalued. I guess I should not be too surprised. Today is really no different than any other day. For the better part of this new millennium, I have been coming to work each day with the same blasé attitude. To be honest, I am not quite sure why I am still working here, other than I really don't think I could go anywhere else. Who would hire me? I have been working in just about the same job, in just about the same company, for the better part of two decades.

Every day when I come to work, the first thing I do is turn on my computer. It's a corporate policy these days. And every day when I follow the corporate policy there are at least, and I am not exaggerating, 500 new emails. Well maybe I am exaggerating a little. But you get the picture. I think there is an organized band of emailers secretly tucked away in their cubicles who keep their index finger permanently adhered to their mouse and click Send, Send, Send, Forward, Forward, Forward all day long. There might even be a subgroup of this cyber-sending club that red-flags every message as Important or Urgent! Here's a novel idea, how about we make a pact to only send

Important and Urgent messages to begin with and hit Delete, Delete, Delete more often.

The head of our IT department, I mean our CIO (not to be confused with our CEO, CFO, COO, CMO, or even our CLO), is probably a technological genius. Every once in a while I see him walking around the building. He looks like the quintessential computer nerd; an inch taller than me, slight body, thick, black, plastic-rimmed glasses, in need of a good tailor, old enough to vote—but not old enough to buy alcohol. One noticeable difference between the usual computer nerd and our CIO is that he lacks a plastic pocket-protector. I am guessing the reason he does not have a pocket protector is because he has no need for pens as all his "writing" is keystroked. He never speaks to anyone and I imagine it would be difficult for him to know if anyone wanted to speak with him as his head appears locked in a downward bow. In spite of the fact that such a perpetually stooped posture is ideal for searching for loose change on the sidewalk, Mr. CIO apparently chooses to forgo the extra income to keep his eyes transfixed to his brand-new highest of all high-speed tablet computer.

I have thought of tapping him on the shoulder to see if his head would automatically spring up but I fear I might startle him and cause a whiplash. And yet, I must give Mr. CIO the credit he is due. He is, most certainly, quite prolific at sending one way email messages. He regularly sends out information about systems upgrades and new programs with which we are to "become familiar." Personally, I don't want to become familiar with new programs. And if you ask me, which no one ever does, the old programs work perfectly and needn't be discarded or replaced.

To tell the truth, I have not always felt this way. In fact, it used to be that I could not wait to get to work. Actually, almost as long as I can remember, I dreamed of working here. Well maybe not working here in the truest sense like contributing to the company's bottom line or performing the duties outlined in my job description, but I did want to work in this office.

You see, when I was in elementary school, in the sixth grade to be exact, I would walk to school. Every day at 8:15 in the morning and then again at 3:15 in the afternoon I would pass right in front of this building; that is if I got out of bed the first time my mother called me in the morning so I was on time for roll call or wasn't delayed by a period of detention in the afternoon for forgetting my homework or wearing make-up. As a four-foot eight-inch tall, seventy-six pound, metal-wired braces, training-bra wearing eleven year old, I was not overly impressed by the architecture of the stately, old, historic brownstone dating back to the 19th century that housed the office, nor was I interested in the type of commerce transacting inside. I was, however, quite smitten by the guy who sat at the desk positioned in front of one of the huge double-hung wooden windows facing out to the street.

Each school day, regardless of the lesson being taught, I was daydreaming and counting down the minutes when I would once again be able to gaze through the office window and catch a glimpse of the dreamboat who had become the love of my life.

It was no surprise he captured my heart. He was my ideal. Picture Vinnie Barbarino, a six-foot tall perfect male specimen, complete with wavy, dark-brown hair and an unmatched sense of suaveness. He wore a perfectly tailored double-breasted gabardine, olive green, three-piece suit with a cream-colored shirt and a maroon striped power tie. His brown leather penny loafers were buffed and polished and even the copper pennies were brushed clean. He was dressed for success, as they say. He actually looked smart. And although I had never seen my dearest love standing up or out from behind his desk, I was confident I had him pegged correctly. He simply set my heart aflutter.

By my estimates he was about ten years my senior. Even though I was no real math wiz, I was able to calculate that if I was hired when I completed my education my heartthrob would be around thirty. Admittedly, I would be reluctant to trust anyone over the age of thirty, but for my "Vinnie" I would make an exception. We would be together, he would sit in his window working diligently and looking so handsome. I would be working at the adjacent desk in front of the adjacent window and looking equally as pretty. From time to time we would steal a loving gaze and share an adoring smile. We would work together, play tennis together, laugh at sitcoms together and even socialize with friends at the bowling alley together. We would always be together. People would say we were the perfect couple. And we would live happily ever after.

Well, not too surprisingly, all things did not work out quite as I had fantasized. I did earn my

Associates degree. My degree enabled me to apply for any job in town and not be qualified for any job in particular. But within two months I was hired by the bank I had set my sights on years before. I was an "assistant to an account manager." I had absolutely no idea what an account manager was let alone what an account manager did. Yet, I was eager to assist. Over time, I learned the "administrative duties" for which I was responsible and the tasks closely resembled those of a secretary.

By the time I started to work in the stately old brownstone office building, the large double-hung wooden windows had been "updated" with smaller vinyl replacement windows. Such a change in the facade allowed for no one to have intimate access to the front windows; absolutely no one, not "Vinnie" and definitely not me.

My semi-private office was on the second floor toward the rear of the building. It was quite warm in the summer as there was no air conditioning and it was equally as cold in the winter because of the antiquated heating system. I shared a 12 x 12 foot space with another newly hired and equally naive assistant to an account manager, Margaret Virginia

Stephanie McCarthy, aka Margie. We were given two metal desks apparently rescued from the army surplus store, two functioning office chairs with wheels that occasionally fell off, two nonfunctioning, totally worthless office chairs that should have been trashed but were being stored "just in case," five partially rusted steel storage cabinets crammed with manila colored files, a closet with cleaning and office supplies, one photocopy machine known to jam after each successful reproduction, and two brand new IBM Executive Electric Typewriters which were the "embodiment of ease, speed, and quality." It was grand! I had arrived!

I must confess that between the sixth grade and the time I got my dream job, my pre through post-pubescent hormones led me to take comfort with other heartthrobs and eventually replace my "Vinnie." And yet when I settled into my work routine and felt comfortable walking around the building by myself, I did go looking for him. I discreetly asked one of the old-timers, Mrs. Kirkland, about my fantasy man.

Mrs. Kirkland was one of those people who naturally lacked a first name, like Mr. Rogers or Captain Kangaroo. The entire time I worked with her I had never heard anyone, not one person from the bottom of the organizational chart to the very top, call her anything other than Mrs. Kirkland. At the time, Margie and I were convinced the four-foot ten-inch tall, ninety-nine pound, salt and peppered haired, woman who was usually dressed in a navy blue or dark grey mid-calf length dress with a white peter-pan collar was one of the original inhabitants of the century old structure who actually knew the brownstone masons and literally came with the building. She was there when we arrived in the morning and was still there when we left in the evening. Mrs. Kirkland was always there. Her desk was perched at the top of the second-floor staircase on a balcony overlooking the main floor. This gave her a clear view of whatever was happening on the first floor as well as what could be happening on the second floor as anyone and everyone who moved vertically in the building had to pass by her desk. I don't know about the other people but I never witnessed Mrs. Kirkland go down or come up the floral patterned carpeted steps that separated the lower from the upper level. Margie and I concluded, probably erroneously, that because of her advanced years and seemingly frail stature, she simply lived at the bank.

Perhaps because Margie and I were all-knowing and wise at this time in our lives, we feared Mrs. Kirkland. In retrospect, she never did or said anything that would have made either one of us afraid. We used her as our "go-to" as most of the other employees did as well. She was extremely knowledgeable about all the forms and required documentation, especially the ones for which Margie and I were responsible. And since she never moved from her desk, she was always available to answer our questions no matter how fundamental (and idiotic) they may have been. Whenever Margie or I, or anyone for that matter, approached her desk she would interrupt whatever she was working on and extend her undivided attention. And although she probably was privy to a lot of juicy details about all of the employees, I never once knew her to be the originating source of sensational rumors. Nevertheless, she scared the living daylights out of Margie and me.

Mrs. Kirkland informed me that the "gentleman of whom you are inquiring is indeed married to a lovely woman, actually a former customer of ours. They have two beautiful children—one boy and one girl." She paused as if waiting for me to ask a follow-up question as she apparently was not going to offer additional information unless I asked her specifically. Perhaps she did not want to appear gossipy. Or maybe I was annoying her. It took a lot of my nerve to just approach her and I froze after she responded so quickly to my question. I stood silently in front of her desk. My eyes fell in a stare to her desk nameplate which read, "Mrs. Kirkland." I tuned her out for a moment and felt a short pang of despair in my gut and wondered how could "Vinnie" do this to me? If he could only see me now; I am all grown up, five feet five inches tall, 118 pounds, shoulder-length layered auburn hair with side-swept bangs to add shape around my face, and straight teeth. My perky boobs fit comfortably into my 34B cup bra while my short skirt and high heels are well balanced with a stylish shoulder padded Christian Dior knock-off blazer. I can drink whatever I want. I can eat whatever and however much I want and never gain an ounce. I can vote, drive at night, date, stay out to all hours or not come home if I don't want to. I can come, go, and do as I damn well please. Not to mention that I am financially independent and drawing a steady paycheck of one hundred and fifty take-home dollars each week.

The slight discomfort in my stomach eased as I snapped out of my self-indulgent, self-imposed, temporary coma. I disconnected my eyes from Mrs. Kirkland's nameplate and politely responded, "Oh, thank you Mrs. Kirkland." I turned away from the old woman and started down the hallway toward my office. I had not taken more than ten steps before Mrs. Kirkland called for me to return to her desk side. She said she wanted me to know, in case I was not aware, and that she was proud to tell me, "That he still works with the company. At another branch, of course. But he is still with us." And then she confirmed, much to my dismay, that his name was not then, is not now, nor has it ever been, "Vinnie."

To be honest, I figured as much. When I got back to my office, I told Margie about my discovery. We shared a giggle and resumed our busy work within the confines of our overly cluttered yet extremely cozy second floor office.

Ah...those glory days! Bruce is so right when he sings, "they'll pass you by in the wink of a young girl's eye." Today is not so glorious. Actually I have not had a glorious day in quite a while. Lots of changes going on constantly. People get hired, people get fired, people just leave whenever they're tired. I am still trying to figure out how Margie and I all of a sudden became the "veteran" staff.

Now my office, or should I say my workstation cubicle, is located downstairs in a regularly reconfigured area in the center of the floor. All four of us account managers, Margie, me, and two girls, recently hired, with no prior work experience, but who have their MBA's and so earn as much if not more than we do with decades of experience and company loyalty, are corralled in the same floor space separated only by what our district manager describes as "lightweight and water-repellant panels that welcome post-its and thumb tacks provided no personal photos are displayed."

The carpeted staircase and balcony are gone. A recent interior remodel included putting floor to ceiling sheet rock over the area and painting it white. Now, only corporate personnel (the "C" team) occupy the second floor which they access via an elevator from the newly constructed rear parking garage.

The connection or should I say the disconnection between the upper level and the lower level extends beyond the physical constructs. Rarely are "they" spotted milling around the lower level with "us" as everyone used to do when I first started working here. And rarely is any communication from "them" to "us" in any other form than electronic.

At times, getting involved in my work can be a struggle as it really does not seem to matter to anyone. Some days it is even difficult for me to get out of bed in the morning. Today is one of those days. I am disinterested and tired. To keep my head from crashing into my computer keyboard, I prop my elbows up on my desk and bury my face in my palms. I close my eyes and try to escape for just a few minutes.

I flash back to Mrs. Kirkland. If she could see me now, she definitely would not approve. Fortunately for me, she can't see me. She does not work here anymore. Ten years ago, when our community bank merged or more accurately was gobbled up by a faceless regional financial institution, Mrs. Kirkland "retired." She was only sixty-four years old. Only sixty-four, who knew?

Whenever I get too comfortably nestled at my desk, I work really hard at not breathing too deeply to generate a snort or grunt. I figure that even the slightest snore probably would not be considered acceptable behavior and who knows, may even cost me an incremental point or two on my annual performance evaluation. I can see it now. My-newly appointed, rarely-visible supervising district manager who I am betting is just a few years removed from taking her 'N Sync posters off her bedroom wall, would dutifully document, "Employee is unengaged. She is disturbing other unengaged employees with her snoring. Recommend the use of medicated nasal strips to clear air passages and follow-up coaching to ensure consistent use."

When my moronic thoughts finally merge with my reality, I raise my head and assume the engaged-employee position. Applying our recent ergonomics training tips, I adjust my seat height, put my feet flat on the floor, tilt my computer monitor, position my source documents, and settle my finger-tips on the home keys with thumbs resting only so gently on the space bar. Then I reach for my super-sized high octane coffee and pray I will have enough energy to make it to lunchtime. With my head slightly cocked and my no-spill insulated coffee travel mug pressed to my lips, I can easily view my computer screen. And just as easily I can see twenty unopened emails in my inbox. With my head still slightly angled I catch a glimpse of my cell phone, strategically positioned next to my monitor. I see five unanswered text messages and four missed calls alert. No surprise. A lot always seems to happen whenever I try to catch forty winks.

Margie peeks her head around the partition to see if I want to join her for a short break. She quips, "Remember what Dickiedo used to say about staring at a computer screen too long." Her chin drops, her face puffs up a bit, and her voice deepens to a bass pitch, "Ultimately it will contribute to eyestrain and tired eyes. Make sure you rest your eyes regularly to reduce fatigue."

Her imitation of Dickiedo is spot on. Former bank president, Mr. Richard P. Doolittle, III, or "Dickiedo" to Margie and me, was our white-haired, always impeccably dressed, horn-rimmed glasses wearing benevolent leader the first year we came aboard. He served as president for decades before we were hired and like Mrs. Kirkland "retired" shortly after the inquisition—I mean acquisition.

Margie and I were on the job for only a few months when he called the full staff together. He stood at the top of the balcony, spread his arms a bit wider than his relatively large body frame, and with hands grasping the thick mahogany railing for support or affect informed everyone in his powerfully, deep, masculine voice that we, "Should not be surprised to see computers replace typewriters in the very near future." Margie was standing next to me when the breaking news hit. We were bug-eyed and absolutely thrilled to be on the cutting edge of technology. We simply could not wait to have our own computer. When I looked over at Mrs. Kirkland, who of course remained seated at her desk alongside Dickiedo, she seemed to be listening yet appeared emotionless. Margie and I were simply off the charts with giddiness about the prospect. This was going to be so cool.

Now, I would have to say, I am not so giddy. And things are not so cool. Nonstop emails, Ccing, Bccing, instant messaging, texts, pop-ups shouting at me all day long make it almost impossible for me to keep up or get anything of importance accomplished. And it seems that each correspondence creates a different and confusing expectation. For example, yesterday a broadcast email informed everyone that "our paper expenses have skyrocketed over the past year." We were "asked" to be "cognizant of our paper usage and go green whenever possible." Today, less than 24 hours later, each cubicle occupant was given a two-page written memo to that effect, to post on our cardboard wall. I wonder what good old Dickiedo would think of the pure nonsense.

I guess Margie grew restless waiting and left for a break leaving me alone with my thoughts. My pensiveness is short-lived as the phone on my desk is having a convulsion. The panel of lights starts flashing and the harsh sounding ring is yelling "Urgent! Urgent! Pick me, pick me!" While I am wishing I could change the ringtone to a soothing ocean wave, I snatch up the receiver to stop the cacophony. Even before I have the opportunity to say hello, I hear the leftover southern drawl of a woman on the other end, "Hey, this is Kitty. I have been trying to reach you. How about we go to the country club for lunch today?"

If I had the chance to respond via text, I would have needed only two letters to get my point across—NW! Saying "no way" to a real live person is a bit more difficult. So instead, "sure, what time?" spontaneously rolls out of my mouth.

I am fortunate to have a friend like Kitty. She is a good friend, a real friend. We have known each other for almost twenty years. We met on a cruise. I am not an enthusiastic seafarer but my husband at the time surprised me with tickets. Besides the toilet backing up in our cabin, we had a lot of fun. I think one of the reasons we had such a good time was that we met Kitty and her highly intelligent husband, Bob. Ever since, Kitty and I have kept in contact. Every once in a while we will "do lunch" and then visit the nail salon. Several years ago, when I was going through my divorce, Kitty unselfishly made herself available no matter what time of the day or night I called her to talk about my idiot ex. Kitty has had a membership at the country club for years. Although I am unsure how she affords it, she goes there for lunch quite often and it is the only restaurant we frequent when it is her turn to treat.

Right before it is time to leave the office to meet Kitty, I go into the restroom to freshen up. I wash my hands with real water instead of hand sanitizer. I apply another layer of super-duper liquid foundation to my face. I use my imitation fiber blush brush to repaint rosy checks. I brandish a no-gunk mascara wand, that is pretty gunky, to thicken and lengthen my thin, short eyelashes. I plumb my collagen-deficient lips with liner and gloss and run my tongue over my front teeth to wipe away any collateral lipstick damage. I comb my hair and tie it back with a plastic barrette. I then take out the barrette and shake my hair to see if the informal look is better. I put the barrette back in. I step back from the mirror for the final panoramic view. I lean closer to the mirror and wonder, "Who is this tired old lady looking back at me?" And without waiting for the answer that probably isn't coming anytime soon, I restore my devices of reconstruction to my cosmetic toolkit and shove everything back into my oversized purse. Then, rather reluctantly, I leave for my lunch date.

It is noon. Kitty and I arrive at the country club in separate cars. We meet in the parking lot, adjacent to the pro shop, as planned. When we get out of our cars we offer each other a quick hello, share a gentle embrace, and like Laverne and Shirley, stroll arm in arm down the brick pathway, up the trio of stone stairs to the clubhouse. Kitty seems her usual calm, peaceful self, tastefully dressed, and flashing a beautiful smile. Part of me is still wishing I had declined the invitation.

From the moment we enter the clubhouse, walk through the lobby, and ride the elevator up one flight to the patio dining area, non-stop pleasantries and acknowledgements are exchanged between the meticulously groomed staff and professionally attired members. For the most part, everyone around the country club acts as if they know each other. Members welcome other members with handshakes and air kisses, and treat each other like Hollywood elite strutting on the red carpet. And I, as usual, feel like a cheap ticket holder peaking from behind the bleachers to catch a glimpse of the A-listers.

As we enter the dining area, a member of the wait staff, a woman about my age, obviously expecting us, is prepared with two menus in hand. She meets us with a gracious welcome and ushers us to a table by a window. Perfect! From my thickly cushioned seat, I have a clear view of the impeccably manicured golf course and the vista beyond the club property. Ah...how totally relaxing. I never want to go back to my office cubicle. NEVER, EVER!

My momentary daydream is interrupted by a menu appearing in front of my chest and Kitty's voice confirming our drink order with the waitress. "My friend will have an iced tea. Make hers unsweetened. I would like to have a real iced tea, sweetened of course."

In many ways Kitty and I are quite similar. We are about the same age and share a similar taste in music, clothes, and movies. We both appreciate the Beatles, Bon Jovi, Frank Sinatra, and Broadway hit tunes. We frequent the same designer clothing stores but Kitty actually buys from the retail store. I search the outlets and am not above purchasing knock-offs from street vendors to save a few dollars. And when it comes to movies, neither one of us finds any enjoyment in modern day special effects and eardrum rupturing surround sound. A good storyline, like Schindler's List, always hits the spot. And we like handsome leading men, provided they are entertaining like Al in Scarface, Russell in Gladiator, and Denzel in just about anything. We enjoy chick flicks, romantic comedies, and feel-good movies and will openly weep in any theatre if we are called upon to do so. Kitty and I do not consider ourselves to be "sequalists." We concur that the original of anything is usually better than the revised version—which could explain why we watch just about any black and white movie on the classic movie channel that does not fall within the silent movie genre.

But when it comes to how we drink our iced tea, there is a continental divide that neither one of us is willing to cross. Perhaps Kitty's southern upbringing makes it a sacrilege to modify the ingredients and remove the sugar. I have no such allegiance and prefer to save my calories for bigger and better things, like dessert.

I have always thought that of all the women I have closely associated with through the years, Kitty is the sharpest. I never realized how in tune and perceptive she truly was until today when she approached me with a targeted question even before I had time to fumble through my pocketbook to put my phone ringer on vibrate. "So what is going on with you and work?" Man, her question hit the bull's eye. Not a really deep question, I admit, but it is direct and to the point. And I use it as a perfect segue to suck in as much oxygen as I need to start venting without having to come up for air.

"I hate my job! I hate how I look! I hate how I feel! I hate the people I work with! I hate their app for this and their app for that! I hate it all! On top of that, I am just not feeling good about myself!"

"OK, take a deep breath. I'm listening," Kitty says in a soothing tone. She is obviously taken aback by my outburst and tries to balance my anxiety with her calm.

I follow Kitty's recommendation, inhale and sit back in my chair. Unable to maintain a restful position for more than a few seconds, I again lean forward and nervously whisper, "Do you remember that classic movie Sunset Boulevard?"

Kitty squints and her forehead wrinkles as she inquisitively asks, "You mean that 1950's movie about the fictional has-been movie goddess, Norma Desmond?"

"Yeah, yeah that's the one, Kitty. Gloria Swanson played the lead role. Remember, in the movie the studio executives ostracized her because she was an aged silent screen actress and the film makers had moved on to talkie movies? And then she became somewhat of a piranha and outcast. She even had delusional dreams of a comeback."

"Yes, I remember. A real classic. I think Swanson was nominated for an Academy Award," Kitty muses as if to contribute something to the conversation.

I need to make it perfectly clear to Kitty that I am in no mood to discuss the 1950 Oscars. First I roll my eyes at her. Then I stare at her. And then in a much higher pitched whisper, I snap, "WHATEVER! The people I work with make me feel like I AM Gloria Swanson in Sunset Boulevard."

Just about the same time I finish dumping my anxiety, our iced tea is served. For the first time since being seated, I take a moment and open the elegant, dark green, pleather, bi-fold menu to review the culinary luncheon delights. As I scan each side of the fare, I see French onion soup, crab and brie salad, rotisserie chicken salad sandwich on a croissant, and crab cake. I hear the waitress carefully recite the specials for the day, Manhattan clam chowder and something with cheese and something else grilled. I don't think Kitty is listening. I know I'm not. With a slight hesitation, Kitty orders a chef salad. And with less hesitation, I order the same.

The waitress confirms our orders, removes our menus, and assures us our salads would be served shortly. As soon as the she walks away from our table, Kitty refocuses our conversation, "Hum...sounds like you are a bit stressed, my friend. Do you think your age has something do with how you are feeling and what is going on at work?"

"I KNOW it does, Kitty. Getting older stinks! It's like I don't know who I am anymore. I look in the mirror and I don't recognize the woman staring back at me. At work there is constant change and it becomes harder and harder for me to keep up. I am fearful of what will happen in a few years, months, maybe even days. Oh my, what if they ask me to leave, then what? I couldn't possibly find another job."

Kitty keeps silent. Her response annoys me just like so many things these days. I have to know what is going on in her pretty little head so I utter impulsively, "Don't you ever feel like I'm feeling?"

In all the years I have known Kitty, she rarely acts impulsively. This time is no different. She sits back in her chair and raises her eyebrows as if she is thinking of her best answer. Within a second or two she shakes her head from side to side, "No."

Internally I shout "WHAT?" Externally, I remain silent. After another slightly longer pause Kitty admits, "Not anymore."

Kitty's answer confuses me. "What? You used to feel like your age was a liability and weighing you down and now you are even older and you don't? So, my dear old friend, here's a newsflash, you are not Ms. Benjamin Button. I know you didn't get any younger, so what in the world happened?"

Kitty points to the brooch she is wearing. Actually every time I am in her company she wears the same brooch. Oddly, since we both have a fondness for fine jewelry, I never thought to ask her about it. Perhaps it is because I know I cannot afford the real stuff like she can. Or maybe I just figure she thinks it was one of those pieces of jewelry that goes with all different outfits, like a stylish ring or watch so she wears it all the time.

The brooch is designed with four diamonds, about a half carat each, running horizontally and linked together with a silver chain. Although deep down there may be flaws in the diamonds, to my naked eye, radiating sparkling brilliance is all I can see. I have to admit, the brooch is simply elegant. If I owned one I would wear it every day.

I stare for a second or two and try to figure out of what qualities and features the brooch reminds me. Aha, it comes to me! The brooch's tasteful design resembles a decorative medal, an earned medal to commemorate some type of event or honor. And with that eureka moment, I figure I should have one as I deserve a medal just for getting up in the morning.

I control my joyful discovery and in a less emotional, and lady-like manner comment, "The brooch is lovely."

And then Kitty, with a very subtle and graceful open-handed gesture, motions for me to look around the room. I follow her lead and gaze from one table to the next. And although I had never noticed them before, I now see several women wearing the exact same brooch.

Perhaps Kitty was intuitive enough to read the look of bewilderment on my face or maybe she was just following up on my comment, "Man, what is up with that?"

Just then, Kitty points to a gray-haired, elderly woman sitting at a large round table at the far end of the dining room. Her back is to the window so her seat faces into the dining area giving her a clear view of all that is going on inside the restaurant. The woman is surrounded by several middle-aged adults and a handful of young adults, perhaps family members.

Regardless of the identity of her companions, this woman stands out from the crowd. She is the center of attention. She is absolutely stunning. She has to be in her eighties at least, yet she is perfectly attired from head to toe.

The woman is wearing a silver-gray sweater trimmed with rhinestones. Her slacks are a bit darker gray and are perfectly coordinated to balance the boldness of her sweater. Her silver dangling earrings, multi-strand necklace and all her jewelry is much more dramatic than the average woman her age would usually wear, but for some reason it looks perfect on her. She is even wearing a stylish tam hat which matches her outfit and allows her wavy hair to peek out just enough to show that it is a sophisticated shade of white.

As attractive as this woman is, what really completes her outfit is her brooch. HOLY MACKEREL! It was the same design as Kitty's. Only the octogenarian's is much bigger! Bigger diamonds, bigger setting! Bigger, bigger, bigger! "Geez Louise," I unthinkingly blurt out.

First, Kitty clarifies. "Not Louise, Lucille. Her name is Lucille." And then adds, "I brought you here today to meet her. You need to have lunch with Lucille. Are you up for it?"

Am I up for having lunch with Lucille? What a question. I hear the words Kitty utters and I admirably catch myself before I say, "You are out of your mind. I'm really not fond of breaking bread with, let alone divulging personal matters to a total stranger, especially one old enough to be my mother or maybe even my grandmother."

In my southern friend's world, civility reigns and proper etiquette never goes out of style. And on top of that, I really do not want to hurt her feelings. I remember my manners, use some forethought, remind myself that Kitty is a good friend and control my words so as not to sound too ungrateful for her concern and concede, "OK, but not today."

Admittedly, as the words roll off my lips, I have already begun to strategize some scenario that would allow me to delay, postpone, and then eventually cancel the luncheon date with Lucille. Perhaps Oprah would send me an overnight delivery with a ticket to be an audience member and I would have to go because she was giving away facelifts. And on that stupid thought, our entrees are served.

While we munch on our chef salads, we share our thoughts and opinions about a variety of subjects; my daughter, her grandchildren, my car trouble, her Reike classes, Nero Wolfe mystery novels, migraine headaches, her cat, my dog, etcetera, etcetera, etcetera. The conversation is virtually nonstop and would have driven any self-respecting man into the darkest pit of madness. We glide from one topic to the next with such ease and grace sometimes using only one word to make the transition. We are masterful!

Our lively interchange makes the lunch hour fly by which, much to my disappointment, leaves no time for dessert. Also much to my disappointment, I am unable to come up with a reason not to have lunch with Lucille. I just hope that by now Kitty, with a few glasses of sugary iced tea under her belt, has abandoned her big idea and I am off the hook.

On our way out of the dining room, we stop by Lucille's table as part of the entourage of women and men who do the same thing throughout the lunch hour. Kitty kisses and hugs Lucille and 1 can hear Lucille say in a low tone almost directly into Kitty's ear, "Sure, I would love that."

Kitty introduces me to everyone at the table. In a way I feel as if Kitty is showing me off to them. I harken back to when I was a young mother and I would be so proud to introduce my daughter to my acquaintances while at the same time hoping she would not do something foolish like sticking her finger up her nose before offering a timid wave and hiding behind my skirt.

Today is slightly different. As each person at Lucille's table graciously offers a warm hello, I am proud to say that I am less shy and more sanitary. I acknowledge each person with a reciprocating smile and friendly, "It's very nice to meet you." And then with no further introduction, Lucille looks directly at me and says in an uplifting and very pleasant voice, "See you Monday, babe."

OMG - Kitty was serious! Oh my goodness, she has followed through with her subversive suggestion! I didn't even get the chance to come up with a good excuse. Kitty has just gone ahead and arranged for my lunch with Lucille. I feel a jabbing pain in my stomach similar to adolescent menstrual cramps. As Kitty and I exit the dining area, I say nothing. The masterful communicator is speechless.

By the time we reach our parked cars my head is spinning just thinking about what is in store for me. Kitty reassures me that spending some time with Lucille will be one of the best things that has ever happened to me. I stand next to the driver's side of her car as she opens the door, positions herself in the driver's seat, buckles her seatbelt and prepares to drive away. She gives me one last smile for the day and says, "Enjoy your lunch with Lucille."

After her good-bye, I realize I am standing alone in the parking lot. There are rows and rows of cars but no people. Not one person anywhere in sight. I feel alone. I stare at Kitty's taillights as her car moves slowly down the country club's long and winding driveway. To be honest, I am not thrilled with what Kitty did. Nor do I understand why she did it. I really don't want to spend my lunch hour with some little old lady. What if Oprah calls?

I reach in my pocket, pull out my keys, and open my car door. I sit behind the steering wheel for a full minute before I start the engine. I try to reconcile what just happened with Lucille and Kitty and what this means to me. At this point, I really don't have a clue. If I could only have a second opportunity to RSVP, I could decline the invitation. But now I have no way out. I will have to have lunch with Lucille. Oh well, at least she will know who Gloria Swanson was.

Annarose Ingarra-Milch

1st DIAMOND

Over the weekend I do my usual chores. I shop for groceries, mop the floors, vacuum the carpets, change the bed sheets, scrub the toilet, and wash the laundry. I have a routine of cleaning my house over the weekend so I can more easily mess it up during the week before and after work. When my chores are done, I plop down on the sofa to watch television. I channel surf for a while and discover the old movie *The Night of the Living Dead*. It is in progress and I have already seen it in its entirety several times. I stop clicking to watch the scene where the bloodthirsty zombies rise from their graves and plod together in the same direction across the cemetery in their shredded, filthy burial outfits looking for food, which of course is in the form of living people. Step by step the risen deceased mindlessly move forward, never speaking to the ghouls to their left or right. No matter how many times I have watched that scene it scares me. It reminds me of people I see every day who walk hunched over with eyes fixated on their mobile devices. That's a scary sight too.

All day Saturday and Sunday I am hoping Monday will never come. But just my luck, it rolls around again. Kitty has arranged for me to have lunch with Lucille at the country club and I am simply not in the mood. In fact, I am not in the mood to do much of anything these days, except eat, of course. Come to think of it, I have always enjoyed eating. And for many years, I could eat whatever I wanted and however much I wanted. My five feet five-inch average frame easily accommodated my 118 pounds. When I was pregnant with my daughter, I had a license to eat, so I maximized my authority and gained forty pounds. After my daughter was born, I dropped twenty pounds without much effort. The other twenty pounds have found a permanent home in my stomach, thighs, and backside. And now that menopause is staring me in the eyeballs, I have been known to play with a few more pounds depending on the time of the year.

It is not that I haven't tried to lose the weight, quite the contrary. I am always trying to lose the weight. I have shaked, juiced, cut carbs, counted calories and even, on the advice of my sister-in-law who swore it worked for her, had a colonic cleansing. It just seems that every time I lose a few pounds, they find me again, like they are attached to a GPS system or something. At times my body shape depresses me. But a good pair of Spanx is my anti-depressant.

The other day I was in a department store dressing room trying on a pair of jeans. I slipped off my shoes and slacks and slipped on the vanity sized jeans. While standing on my tippy toes, because the jeans were five inches too long for me, I held up my shirt so I could see if my tummy bulged when the jeans were fully zipped and buttoned. I turned to the left and yanked them up. I turned to the right and smoothed them down. I turned around and squatted down to see if there was enough room in the seat. Then I looked straight on in the mirror at my face wondering if the image was real. It's not that I don't look at myself in the mirror at home every day because I do. I primp and preen as much as the next woman. It's just that my mall reflection seemed so much more revealing. In the bright light, the circles under my eyes seemed to have darkened and my skin tone looked a lot less even. Even the lines around my mouth have multiplied. What the heck is going on? Do they make Spanx for the face?

Last week, my co-worker "little Ms. MBA" commented that my "glabella" is deep. Although at first I thought she was paying me a compliment, I quickly realized from whence it came and sensed it was not a good thing. I told my co-worker I was going to look up the word "glabella" in the dictionary; she wisecracked, "Google it." I did and discovered that it is the area between the eyebrows. Who knew my doe-eyed, genius co-worker learned about anatomy in MBA school. Thing is, she was right. My glabella is deep. In fact my glabella is an inch-long crevice with a depth of at least one fathom, strategically centered to divide my face in half. Maybe that's where the expression "two faced" comes from.

Throughout my morning at work I am preoccupied with thoughts of today's lunch. I do manage to process some paperwork and respond to a dozen emails but as the noon hour approaches, I grow more and more apprehensive about the upcoming tête-à-tête. I figure if I want to spend my lunchtime with the elderly, I'll volunteer at the rest home. I am not feeling the usual warm fuzzies about my friend Kitty, either; she has it all, diamond jewelry, country club membership, a doting husband and now, rather than spend time with me, she sets me up with a little old lady.

Before leaving work for my dreaded lunch, I stop into the restroom to freshen up. As I wash my hands, I look up and see my reflection. Damn! I am going to start a movement to rid the world of mirrors. But not today. I have a lunch meeting. I remind myself to add "ban the mirror movement" to my to-do list and leave for the country club.

Always a good time manager, I arrive at the country club shortly before the noon witching hour. I park by the pro shop, walk down the brick pathway, to the three stone stairs, enter the clubhouse, and take the elevator up one flight. En route I pass a few club members. One or two acknowledge my existence with a perfunctory nod. A few others ignore me all together. I guess they are aware they don't know me because I am well aware that I don't know them.

As I make my way into the dining room, there sits Lucille; positioned at the same table she was last week when I met her. And just like last week she is sitting with her back to the window, the beautiful golf course scene serving as her backdrop, as she looks out into the dining area.

Although there are several-dozen other members in the restaurant, Lucille stands out. She looks like a model; not a runway model as she does not have the slender bone structure and I doubt she is anywhere near tall enough. Instead she resembles a commercial or print model. Her body is well-proportioned, her face is quite attractive, and her skin is astonishingly silky, especially for a woman of her advanced years. My first impression is that Lucille, with minimal airbrushing, is worthy of a cover shot on some mature lifestyle focused magazine.

Even if I had really poor eyesight, which I do not, I would not be able to miss Lucille. She is illuminated. From head to toe, she is fully adorned in aquamarine. Her blouse, her pants, her scarf, and all of her jewelry show some shade of the blue hue. I have never seen anything like it! Her aquamarine-colored hat reminds me of the pee cap John Lennon wore when the Beatles first landed in New York in 1964; only Lucille has it strategically tipped to one side, just enough to expose her gleaming white hair.

As I near Lucille's table, I notice her aquamarine blouse is also trimmed in sequins. And there, perfectly positioned over her heart, is the four-diamond brooch, at least twice as big as Kitty's. It shines so brightly and almost appears happy to see me.

But what radiates even more than the four diamonds is Lucille's smile. She follows me with her eyes as I walk unceremoniously through the dining room. Her grin grows progressively broader. Seemingly, she becomes increasingly more joyful with every step I take in her direction.

I feel assured there is no way I can go off course. Lucille's smile is reeling me in like a helpless fish. I walk directly to her table and sit down next to her. Trying to sound confident, I say "Hi Lucille." In reality, I am praying she remembers me. She looks over at me, beaming with delight, as if she's known me all her life and is thrilled that I am joining her. She touches my hand and enthusiastically greets me, "Hi ya babe, good to see you."

And with that sincere reception, I feel an immediate sense of belonging. Since I have been joining Kitty at the club, I have always felt like an outsider. It really is not that surprising. After all, I am an outsider, a visitor, a guest or to others maybe even an interloper. Now, in the few seconds I am sitting with Lucille, she extends such a genuine welcome that I can feel my sense of discomfort fade away.

The waitress visits our table. She is the same server who attended to Kitty and me last week. This time, instead of handing Lucille and me each a menu, she greets Lucille and simply rattles off the day's specials. "We have a few different appetizers today that you might like. We have oysters on the half shell, prosciutto-wrapped scallops, and potato pancakes topped with a dollop of sour cream and dill. For entrees we have Fusilli pasta with shrimp, beef brisket, thinly sliced and garnished with tomatoes and parsley." Before she has the opportunity to add another delight, Lucille interrupts her. Apparently Lucille knew what she wanted way before the waitress began her dissertation. "I will have a cup of pea soup and an open grilled cheese sandwich on rye." It all happened so quickly that I simply agree, "me too" just so as not to hold up the process.

"OK then, two cups of pea soup and two open grilled cheese sandwiches on rye. Is there a specific type of cheese you would like?"

Lucille thinks for one second, "Swiss." "Me too," I say. Again I did not want to delay the order. And besides, I like Swiss cheese.

Before the waitress leaves the table, she looks at Lucille and asks, "What would you like to drink today, Lucille?"

Again, Lucille does not think too long or hard about her choices as it seems she was only waiting to be asked, "Today, I will have a Jack Daniel's on the rocks with a twist."

"A twist or a wedge of lemon?" They both chuckle. I guess it is an inside joke. Lucille declares, "You are so smart, a wedge as usual."

Wow! Jack Daniel's! I thought Lucille would be an Earl Gray tea drinker. I order an iced tea—unsweetened, of course. I really want a Jack too, but it is a bit too early in the day for me and I have to get back to the office.

The waitress walks away from our table smiling. Lucille looks at me and winks. Her abrupt eyelid movement exposes aquamarine eye shadow, which, of course, matches her entire outfit. How strikingly creative for a woman her age!

I simply have to comment. "Lucille, you look so lovely dressed all in blue."

"That is very kind of you to tell me."

Accepting compliments has never been my forte. Staying true to form, I ignore Lucille's gracious words and go right on talking. "Lucille, you are so blue all over. Do you ever get blue?"

"Not really. Do you?" Lucille responds without giving my question much time for consideration.

I hesitate a bit and then I hear my voice drop as I admit, "Yes, it seems a lot these days."

With a softness and almost maternal concern in her voice, Lucille asks, "Do you think there is something physically wrong with you? My son is a really good doctor. Do you think you need to see a doctor?"

Lucille's empathetic display of concern for my well-being startles me. I hardly know this woman. Why is she expressing interest in me? "No, no. I go to my doctor regularly. I am quite physically healthy."

Lucille looks at me sporting a big grin, "That is absolutely awesome! My grandson taught me that word 'awesome.' It really comes in handy in certain situations like now, for example. You tell me that you are physically healthy and I can honestly say, 'awesome.' Do you think that is awesome?"

"Well, I never really thought of it like that. I guess it is awesome that I am physically OK," I reluctantly admit.

"Yes, I am glad you agree that good health is awesome because good health is truly awesome," she says, with an emphatic tone in her voice and stressing the words and the link between "good health" and "truly awesome."

When she is convinced she has gotten her point across, she asks, "Then why do you think you get blue?"

"So many things...where should I start?" I mumble half-heartedly hoping she won't hear me.

Instead of backing off, Lucille leans in closer to me perhaps to convince me that she is truly listening to every word, including my mumbo jumbo. And without skipping a beat, she does her best imitation of Julie Andrews from *The Sound of Music* and begins to sing, "Let's start at the very beginning, a very good place to start."

Oh my! Stop the music, please! How strange is that behavior? Is she losing her mind? Is she just being goofy to put me at ease? How am I supposed to espouse all my woes to some little old lady when I feel so embarrassed—for both of us?

The best response I can muster while hoping she will drop the interrogation or at least change the subject is, "Not important." But I soon realize Lucille is not going to let me off the hook that easily. She presses on.

"Sure they are, babe. They are important to you and that makes them important to me. I want to hear all about what makes you feel blue."

And with Lucille's permission, I say to myself, "you asked for it" and I start rattling, "This aging stuff is getting to me. I look so old. I feel so old. I feel sooo stupid. At work, for example, the gen X'ers and some Y's are difficult for me to work with. The little chippies, each with their MBA's—they just seem to know so much. They have apps for this and apps for that. They scroll while they talk. They text while they walk. They rarely look you in the eye. And they seem to move so fast."

I think I gave Lucille a bit more information than she bargained for. She grabs for my hand and pats it as if to say slow down and interjects, "Wait a minute "X? Y?"

"Sorry about that Lucille," as I realize how fast I am speaking. In a way, I guess I am relating to Lucille the way X & Y relate to me.

I explain, "Gen X and Y are people born in the 70's through the 90's. About half the people I work with fall into that age range."

"Who is in the other half?"

"The other half are boomers, like me. People, predominately women in their 40's, 50's and 60's."

"All youngsters!"

I guess from her perspective we are all youngsters. Maybe that is why she keeps calling me "babe."

Lucille follows up with two questions. "What makes you feel so old and stupid, as you say? What is it that X and Y know that you do not know?"

Once again, I feel as if Lucille is giving me permission to rant. So I offer her a litany of all the technological advances and nouveau lingo that goes on in the office.

"Let's see. We have bits and bytes and chips and discs, iPads, iPhones, iPods. We have pipelines, power sources, PRAM, Ethernet and internet, IT, ISP, ISO, ISA not to mention encoding, debugging and spyware, which is not to be confused with malware. And then there are always micros and macros, file extensions and file formats. I log in and I log out. I protect against viruses, worms and of course the Trojan Horse."

Lucille's head is bobbing up and down. Her hat remains in position. Her face has a look of bewilderment. While she tries to wrap her brain around the Trojan Horse concept, I keep firing. "We used to be reengineering, then we were downsizing, and now we are right sizing. Once we were concerned with outsourcing and now we are focused on insourcing. And we no longer are off-shoring, because now we are looking at re-shoring. We have synergic relationships, which of course are win-win. Everything we do must be value-added and customer centric, while aligning with corporate strategies."

Lucille calls for a cease-fire, "Wait a minute. Do you even know what you are talking about?"

"Not really," I admit, almost out of breath.

"That's TMB, babe."

I think for a second to see if I recognize the trio of letters. "What, TMB? I must have missed that acronym."

"Too Much Baloney. I just made it up."

Obviously Lucille has heard enough. We share a laugh but it is short-lived as Lucille wants to know how I feel about all the "baloney".

I take a moment to think, but deep down I already know how it makes me feel. "Quite frankly Lucille, I feel as if it is all going on around me and without me."

"Hum... interesting. Do you feel like you are being left behind or left out? Like you used to feel so smart and now you feel so stupid."

"Exactly!"

"Have you always felt this way?"

My quick response is, "I don't think so" followed with a more emphatic, "No, definitely not. When I was first hired as an assistant account manager, I didn't know anything about the business. My supervisors spoke with me, showed me what to do, and answered my questions. Come to think of it, I felt more like I was being pulled along, as opposed to feeling left behind. I felt included."

"So now you feel more excluded?"

I hear my voice quiver just a bit, as I confess, "Yes. That is one way to put it, Lucille. I feel unimportant and—at times—invisible."

Lucille's maternal instinct doesn't kick in. I know she hears the tremble in my voice but she chooses to ignore it. She refuses to allow me any time to wallow. "So, what do you do when Casper the friendly ghost takes you over?"

"Well, sometimes I get depressed."

"I would probably feel the same, babe. It is horrible to feel overlooked."

Lucille finally exposes her motherly side and I'm appreciative. Once my feelings are validated, it is easy to continue. "But you know what Lucille, mostly I get so freakin pissed off...oops, excuse my French." I can't believe I said that in front of Lucille.

"Is that French? I have some better Italian words you could use," she says totally unaffected by my slip of the tongue and coaxes me to continue. "And then..."

"And then I raise my voice to ensure they hear me or I go to the other extreme and hide in my cubicle and give everyone the silent treatment. And then when Margie, Margie is my colleague and friend, and I get together I talk about how disrespectful they are and how childish they act. I have even been known to shoot off an email, or two or three, that I later regret sending. And then...I get so mad at myself for acting like that."

"Sounds like your really beat up on poor babe. Why do you get so mad at yourself for acting like that?'

"Because, it is not who I am. I really am not an angry, gossiping witch."

Lucille raises her eyebrows, nods and smiles as if in agreement with me. On second thought maybe her facial expressions are just telling me she has heard it all before. Regardless of her motivation, she continues with a brief and seemingly disconnected inquiry, "You know I am a widow, right?"

OMG! I am talking tech and baring my soul to a woman who wants to reminisce about morbidity. What have I done? What should I do? I feel so stupid. Should I shut up or keep talking? Why can't I think of another "French" word to distract her?

Lucky for me the waitress has impeccable timing. She arrives at our table with our drinks just as Lucille starts to go off on a tangent. As the waitress sets our drinks on the cocktail napkins, Lucille is quick to express her gratitude and congratulations, "Thank you, sweetheart. Look at that beautiful wedge of lemon. Nice job."

And then in the next breath, Lucille lifts her glass to make a toast. "Salute!" she boldly states, "Cent'anni!"

Say what? I refrain from asking Lucille for clarification but Lucille is perceptive and hears in my voice when I try to echo "Cent'anni" or some variation thereof that I have absolutely no idea what I am talking about.

"Do you know what Cent'anni means?"

"No, not really."

"It is a way to wish someone 100 years of good life."

What a nice sentiment. Glad she told me. I will remember that one.

With that lesson under my belt, we each take a sip of our drinks. I have to admit, Lucille appears to be enjoying her Jack more than I am my iced tea. I add two packets of artificial sweetener, stir with my plastic straw, and take another sip. Much better.

I am hoping the brief interruption and our sidebar conversation is enough to take her off the topic of reminiscing about her deceased husband. But just as soon as she swallows her sip of Jack, Lucille picks up exactly where she left off.

"So...I had three children. My husband was a doctor. Did you know that? "

Kitty had told me bits and pieces about Lucille's life and the only thing I really remember is that she was a doctor's wife, which might explain how she gets to hang out at the country club every day. I didn't confirm or deny that I knew anything about her history, I just sat there listening.

"Anyway, I had worked to put my husband through medical school. After he graduated, he got a job here, right at the local hospital." She points out the window to the golf course. In spite of her apparent mistake, I understand what she means. I figure she either has a poor sense of direction or it isn't an important part of her story as the hospital is located miles away and in a totally different direction than the first tee on the front nine.

She doesn't seem too phased by her mistake and continues with the story. "We moved from the big city to this town where they roll up the sidewalks at night." She pauses to laugh at what she considers to be a joke and takes a sip of Jack. "I stayed behind in the city for awhile as I didn't want to move over 100 miles from everyone in my family. You know, I came from a really big family. I had seventeen brothers and sisters. I am the youngest!" she proudly declares as she bats her eyes and turns her right index finger 180 degrees into her imaginary dimple to make cutesy like Shirley Temple.

We share a short laugh and each take another sip of our drinks. Lucille continues, "My husband was a doctor. He went back to school later in life. There was a war and all, you know. He didn't serve in the war, though. He tried to enlist but he walked with a limp so he was excused, at least for a while. That's another long story. We had been married a very short time when my husband decided that since he couldn't join the army, he was going to go back to school and become a doctor."

As I get ready to ask how she felt when her husband made the decision to return to school, apparently without her input, Lucille takes a serious gulp of Jack, a deep breath, and with firmness in her voice, moves on with the story.

"You know, babe, I was flabbergasted. Absolutely flabbergasted! Keep in mind, things were different then. Back in the 1940's it was not common, actually it was extremely rare, that an older adult, a married man, would quit a job and depend on the support of his wife to go back to school to change careers. And that is exactly what I told him—in my own way."

She raises her right hand slightly off the table and cups the tips of her fingers all together. She motions them back and forth, matching her words with the fluid rhythm of her hand gesture and emphatically declares, "Tu sei pazzo, Tu sei pazzo, Tu sei pazzo!"

I used to be a fan of the television show, The Sopranos. I think it was Tony who used the expression "pazzo." I am pretty sure it means crazy. And I had seen Little Paulie and Big Pussy make the same expressive hand gesture as Lucille so I am able to follow Lucille's script. She adds a few more choice Italian words with such passion that I doubt they would have passed the TV censors. Admittedly, I don't understand the other foreign words and phrases but her forceful tone and glaring facial expressions unmistakably convey her disapproving message.

"Oh boy," Lucille continues without calming down, "And then I reminded him that he was out of school for so many years and that he was so much older than the other college students, and then I questioned how the hell was he going to keep up with all those youngsters?"

I sense Lucille is feeling a bit agitated, to put it mildly, as she recalls how she felt that day so many years ago when her husband broke the news to her that he was quitting his job and going back to school. I am actually feeling her angst and I really, really, really, wish I had a shot of Jack. Instead, I settle for a sip of my iced tea. Then I lean forward in my chair to hear, as the legendary radio broadcaster Paul Harvey used to say, "the rest of the story."

Lucille reaches for my hand, holds it tightly, and sounding much more in control of her emotions says, "Well babe, my husband took my hand and we sat down on the sofa. He looked in my eyes, and said in a calming, self-confident, and convincing tone, 'I look at it from this perspective Lucille, if they'll teach me, I will learn."

Lucille squeezes my hand harder. I notice she does not take a sip of Jack this time. Instead she diverts her eyes away from me and then back to me with a deep stare right into my eyeballs. After she comes out of her momentary trance, she gives me a short smile as if she is rehearing her husband's prophetic words over and over in her head, "If they'll teach me, I will learn. If they'll teach me, I will learn."

There is a short period of silence that makes me feel uncomfortable. I need to unlock my eyes from Lucille's. I look down and realize her napkin has fallen on the carpet. As I lean over and reach to pick it up, I notice her shoes are patent leather aquamarine. Why would anyone need aquamarine colored shoes?

Without skipping a beat, I hand her the napkin with a compliment attached, "Nice shoes." Lucille responds matter-of-factly, "It's all part of it, babe."

Our eyes lock again. Only this time, it is comforting.

Our server stops by the table and asks if everything is satisfactory. In unison, we answer, "Yes, fine, thank you." She picks up Lucille's swizzle stick and my empty pink artificial sweetener packets from the table, while simultaneously informing us that our soup will be served shortly.

Usually at this time of day, I am famished. By noon, the gastro rumbling begins, followed by a deep guttural growl and a hollow feeling in the pit of my stomach. It doesn't matter if I am brown-bagging it, ordering in, or dining out, every single day at lunchtime, I am starving and I cannot wait to eat. But, today is different. I know it sounds corny but being with Lucille leaves me with a much different hunger and thirst. In fact, I really don't care if I eat or drink anything. Instead, I have an appetite to hear more of her stories, even though I don't have the slightest idea as to why she is telling me all of this.

After the waitress leaves, I sense Lucille is a bit shaken and I don't want to press for any more information, although I have to admit, her story is growing more interesting. Thankfully, she resumes where she left off without any prompting from me. "Babe, I remember that day as if it were yesterday. It was a real defining day for me."

I think, of course, it was. It must have been during that time that her husband went back to school and became a successful doctor. Then they probably moved into a big house, had children, and lived happily ever after. I didn't say what I was thinking because I wanted Lucille to tell me the happy ending herself.

"Well babe, as you probably guessed, my husband got his medical degree and became a successful doctor. We bought a big house. We had three children. And then...and then...and then...he died."

Oh my...that sucks! I was pleased I seized another opportunity to keep my mouth shut, which admittedly is rare for me. And then, trying to sound appropriately respectful, I say, "Oh...I am so sorry to hear that. When did he die?" I was confident Lucille's husband had lived to a ripe old age, like her, leaving her the wealthy widow.

"He died when he was forty years old. I was forty as well. Although I told everyone I was thirty-nine because in those days wives were not to be older than their husbands. Glad that rule changed. Anyway, he had pancreatic cancer. And he died within three months or so after getting sick. Little Joe Cartwright from the Ponderosa had the same disease."

This story jumped the shark. It was now growing increasingly gloomy. I pick up on the Little Joe aspect to distract her, "You mean, Michael Landon from Bonanza?"

"Yes, I watch Bonanza every afternoon at 3:00," Lucille confesses.

And without any hesitation she tells me that when her husband died, she had a big house with a big mortgage and small kids; two boys, nine and six and a daughter four years old.

Then she recollects how she felt. "I was so scared. I was so sad. I kept asking myself, how am I going to support myself and my three kids? I am 40 years old. What am I going to do...what am I going to do? There was very little money because my husband died before his earning potential really took off."

"So what did you do?"

"I guess I did what everyone who experiences a loss does—I cried and cried and cried."

Boy oh boy, that was a really stupid question. I didn't have to ask her that question. I know that feeling—that sense of loss. Shortly after my daughter was born, I had a nightmare that something terrible happened to my husband and I was left alone with my baby with no idea what to do or where to go. It was one of the worst dreams I ever had. Fortunately for me, my daughter's father did not die. But when he walked out on the two of us ten years later, our loss was more than a bad dream. It was a dreadful reality and I was devastated. I remember the bouts of bawling and the lingering loneliness. Part of me wished he was dead. Regardless, I can't imagine the profound depth of Lucille's grief.

Lucille's story is getting progressively sadder and I am beginning to wish she would just end it so the suffering would end as well. But she continues without breaking stride. "And then after a grieving period, I looked at my kids and realized I had a responsibility to them, to make the life for them that my husband and I had planned from the very beginning. And the only way I was going to make that happen was to stop feeling sorry for myself, look at life from a different angle and go back to work."

"Oh my goodness, that must have been frightening. You were a forty-year old woman who had been out of the workforce for over a decade. There was a much younger generation in the workforce, I am sure. And there really weren't a lot of women in the workforce to begin with back then. What skills did you possibly have that would be applicable in the marketplace? Gee, and you were a woman and forty years old!"

"Babe, you are so funny. You make it sound like it was the end of the world for me. In fact, you sound like I did when my husband and I were sitting on the sofa that day when he told me he decided to go to medical school."

Lucille continues, "Let's look at it a different way. It was because I had been through so much, and knew that change happens all the time, I had a much easier time of looking at this chapter in my life not as the end, but rather the beginning of what I needed to do to make a new and rewarding life for me and my kids."

"Of course I was scared about rejoining the workforce after so many years, who the hell wouldn't be? But I was fortunate. I had a reference point. I had a lot of experience. I heard that self-confident voice of my husband so many years earlier when he decided to go back to school. We had been through so many ups and downs and life-altering experiences. I knew how to go with the flow. And I knew how to see this situation from a different perspective."

"I knew it was time. I was beginning to be that powerful woman. Although I could very easily have had a pity party for myself, I chose to see myself as the capable, strong, independent woman that I needed to be."

While listening to Lucille, I try to relate to her sentiments. After my divorce I had mixed emotions. Being capable, strong, and independent were not in the mix. Feelings of regret, anger, weakness, self-doubt, worthlessness, and failure lingered for quite a while. To this day they sometimes still rear their ugly head. At least when I was going through my divorce, I had my work. My co-workers at the time were very supportive and helped me cope. I wonder what I would have done if I did not have my job and had to look for work like Lucille.

Without sounding too much like a Human Resource generalist I ask, "What skills did you have to qualify you for the workforce?"

"I had my high school diploma. And I knew how to type."

"That's it; those were your only qualifications?"

"Of course not. Those were just my jumping off points. I had years of experience."

"Doing what?"

"Living."

"That's comical."

"Really, you think that life experience has little value?"

"No, no that is not what I meant. I just think that we all have experiences, regardless of age."

"That's true. We all, regardless of our age, have some life experience," Lucille concedes.

Then she follows up, "So what happens if you live longer?"

"Well, the more life experiences you would have, I guess."

"Bravo!" she shouts as if I answered the million dollar question. "Yes, the longer you live, the more and varied experiences you have. And the many different situations and life circumstances you live through teach you valuable lessons."

"Yes, I will give you that, Lucille. And that is what you took into your job?"

"You bet. I knew I had valuable job skills. I knew how to do a variety of things and had many talents that were vital to my and any business' success. I knew how to deal with adversity and loss. I knew how to control my emotions. I knew how to get along well with people to build relationships. I knew how to be respectful, how to talk with people and how to work with people. I knew the value of being loyal, patient, and understanding, and of having a sense of humor and being able to laugh at myself. I knew how to use my time wisely, prioritize and easily identify what is truly important and what is not. Through my years I learned life lessons that you cannot learn in school. There is no textbook, no classroom instruction, no other way to learn about life than to live it."

As Lucille was relating her oral resume, I thought, I know those things too.

"Lucille, do you think those skills are needed in today's high tech workplace."

"I admit I have not worked in an office for many years. But I can assure you that people are people and the higher tech you go, the more touch they will crave."

"Perhaps, but from where I sit, people touch screens more than they touch people?"

"And do you know how to touch people?"

"Yes, I think I do."

"So you know things others do not know."

"Yes, I guess I do at that."

I lower my head and in a barely audible voice say "But for the most part, I think they know more than I do." I am unsure if Lucille hears my last comment. She acts rather unfazed. She takes a sip of her drink and continues, "When I went back to work after twenty years a lot of things were different then they were before. They even had a machine that if I stuck my finger in a hole and spun it around several times I could eventually hear the voice of someone far away."

I raise my head and shoot a disoriented look in Lucille's direction.

"I am just kidding. We always had telephones in my workplaces. I just wanted to see if you were listening."

And when she is assured that I am all ears she continues. "The bottom line is this. I knew how to do a lot of things. I didn't know how to do everything. But I was willing to value that which I did not know."

"Just like your husband did."

"Ah, you finished my sentence," Lucille quickly adds.

"So did you feel confident and smart?"

Lucille laughs, "Of course. I was smart. I am smart. I am comfortable with who I am. I am comfortable with being me. That is what smart is. It's self confidence. I am comfortable with what I know and with what I don't know; with what I can do and with what I can't do. I will show you what I know and I am willing to learn whatever it is that I need to learn. I am OK with asking someone to teach me as I am OK with teaching someone else."

After a short pause for another sip of our drinks, Lucille curiously asks, "Do you have an answering machine at your house?"

I really want to know "why" but instead I go with the flow, "No, not anymore. Now I just use my cell phone for all my calls, so my messages go directly into my voice mail."

"Wow that is so exciting! I think it is wonderful to keep up with all the new things that are happening around us. Good for you! Cell phones are a challenge for me to use. They are hard to hear and the buttons are so small. But they are so convenient and keep us connected."

And then without taking another breath Lucille continues, "About 25 years ago my daughter installed my first answering machine. I remember I loved to hear who was thinking of me while I was away from my house."

That is a friendly way of looking at it. I hate my voicemail, especially when the caller talks and talks and talks and never says anything. Lucille seems to have this knack for looking at everything from a different perspective. And usually her perspective is from the positive side.

"Well, within the first week, my daughter called and left a message. I heard her cheerful upbeat voice so plainly, 'Mom if you want to go out to dinner with me this evening, I will pick you up at five o'clock. Let me know.' Of course I wanted to go. I always want to go." She pauses, I am assuming, to make sure I know that about her.

"I was all dressed and ready to go by five. I waited on the porch for my daughter to pick me up but she did not come for me. No one came for me. Not at five, not at six, not even at seven. Jeopardy was on at seven o'clock so I shut out the porch light, poured a glass of wine, and went into my bedroom to watch the show."

"What happened then?" I am figuring this story has to go somewhere.

"Well, just after Alex Trebek completed the Final Jeopardy question, my daughter came in. By this time, I was less mad. A good glass of wine will do that for you. But I was still quite annoyed for being stood up. She had a perky somewhat sassy tone, 'Hi Mom how's Alex doing?' I was thinking that Alex is a lot better than you are going to be because I am going to ring your neck for standing me up."

"Oh my, Lucille, you two must have had some fight," I interject thinking of what would have happened if the situation played out with me and my daughter.

"Actually, babe, instead of jumping all over her, which one side of me wanted to do, I calmly, or at least somewhat calmly, asked why she didn't pick me up. My daughter simply replied, 'Mom I left you a message. You didn't call me back to tell me you wanted to go.'"

"Now get this babe, this is the strangest thing. I thought I did tell her I wanted to go with her. The problem was I was talking to the answering machine. I didn't know I had to actually pick up the phone receiver and call her back. Her voice sounded so real, I could have sworn she was listening. When I explained to my daughter what happened and she explained to me what happened, we both laughed so hard. It would have been a funny sight for someone who was listening, like a fly on the wall, to hear me talking back to the answering machine, 'Sure sweetheart I will go to dinner with you. I will be ready at five. I love you too!' "

"So what, you made a simple mistake Lucille. No big deal."

"Yes I did make a simple mistake, babe, and I did not turn it into a big deal."

"Yeah, you could have ended up in a big fight with your daughter."

"Yes that is true. I could have made it a big deal."

"Glad you two got a good laugh out of it."

"Right again. Laughing turned my mistake into a fun event. So much fun that I am telling you all about it," she says with a ha-ha in her voice.

"I try not to make mistakes."

"Don't try too hard, babe."

"What do you mean by that?"

"Well, if I didn't make the mistake, I would never have learned how to use the answering machine. Right?"

"Yes, I guess so. But I still don't like making mistakes."

"I agree with that. I don't like making mistakes either. I look at mistakes as something I did because I tried, I gave it a shot, took a risk, and then I learned. And then I laughed. That's life. No one knows everything. Sometimes you have to ask for help."

"I am afraid of making mistakes."

"Why are you afraid of making mistakes?"

"I don't like letting people know that I don't know. I think it's a sign of weakness."

"Wow, I guess that is one way to look at it. Do me a favor, babe, and try to flip that thought around. I want to hear what it sounds like upside down."

"OK, let me think for a moment." I pause to try and figure out how to do what Lucille has asked of me.

"Instead of saying I am afraid of making mistakes and I don't like people knowing that I don't know because it makes me look weak, I will flip it and say, I am not afraid of trying. It lets people know I want to learn and it is a sign of strength."

"Much better. Thank you."

Did Lucille just trick me into saying something I did not want to say? Yes, she did. And yet when I said it, it really did make sense. At work especially around Ms. MBA I struggle with admitting I don't know something. I think if I tell her that I don't know something, I will appear less intelligent than her or plain stupid.

"You know people are like diamonds. Just like a diamond has flaws, so do we. And just like a diamond is able to shine, in spite of or because of, its flaws, so can we. And just like a diamond is multi-faceted, so are we. Each of us has different strengths and different shortcomings. You are a very smart woman, babe. You know a lot and can learn a lot."

This time I am a bit more comfortable with the kind words and I accept them graciously. "So do you know how to use the answering machine now?"

"Sure, it's so easy. My daughter gave me a play-by-play. Now I am an answering machine scholar. I even know how to erase messages. I can teach you if you would like." We share the humor in her kooky invitation. Together we raise our glasses and take another sip of our drinks.

"Lucille, you are funny. I see how people can be drawn to you." As I am speaking I can feel myself becoming more and more comfortable in her company. Her insights and light hearted interpretations of real life situations are making this a very interesting lunch hour.

"Thank you for such a nice compliment. I am glad you are having lunch with me today."

While Lucille may be glad I am joining her for lunch, I am truly honored. The longer our conversation goes on, the easier it is for me to understand why Kitty adores her.

Lucille simply exudes self confidence. She knows who she is. She has lived through a lot and more importantly has used what she learned to grow as a person. Now she is teaching me. She is showing me how to do it. The term that comes to mind is "leading by example." She seems to take her role quite seriously while at the same time not taking herself one bit seriously.

Everything she does, even what she wears has her looking the part and acting the part of a woman who knows her strengths and is able to laugh at her weaknesses; I never looked at her that way before. I always saw her as some well-to-do widow born with the proverbial silver spoon in her mouth.

"You know, Lucille, I remember Kitty using a phrase, 'crystallized intelligence'. She defined it as the knowledge and skills we acquire over a lifetime."

Lucille jumps right on it, "I love that term— crystallized intelligence. Did you know diamonds are crystals?"

"I didn't realize that," I say as my eyes fall on her diamond brooch.

"Gives you a new perspective, doesn't it?"

As the soup is being served, I have an epiphany which is quickly interrupted by Lucille asking me to put on her bib. Hello Lady! We aren't at a seafood house why would you wear a bib? And then, just being Lucille so comfortable with herself, she nonchalantly pulls an actual bib from her pocketbook and hands it to me as if I instinctively know what to do with it. It is the same shape as a baby bib only several sizes larger, making it easy to latch around her neck with a small strip of Velcro. Keep in mind this is no ordinary looking bib. Besides its adult size, it is made out of some type of velveteen material and, you guessed it, is aquamarine!

While I am attaching Lucille's velveteen aquamarine bib, it dawns on me that what I do is focus on those skills that I don't have, even to the point of resenting those who do have them. No wonder I feel out-dated, old, and stupid, even valueless. I close myself off so I stop learning. And then I behave in such a way that is really not like me.

Now, if I use my decades of experiences and the countless lessons that have come from them, then my age would hold value. The more age, the more value. How hard could it be to change my perspective and look at my age that way? I am a crystallized intelligent woman, if that is a word. I bet if I did change my perspective, the blues that pop up so often would ease a bit. I am sure I'd feel better about myself and more self-confident. And I could show the people I work with who I really am.

And on that simplistic thought, I reposition myself comfortably in my seat, pick up my spoon and begin to eat my soup.

As the noon lunch hour progresses a steady stream of people parade to our table to pay homage to Lucille. Her mere presence in the dining room attracts members, visitors, and staff of all ages, genders, and ethnicities. The one unifying characteristic of this diverse group is that each individual follows the same ritual when they approach the grand madam. First they extend a polite word and then follow up with a sincere hug and kiss. Lucille introduces me as "her friend" and I shake one hand after another. It is an impressive experience to watch how Lucille so effortlessly commands everyone's full respect and attention. No woman or man in the room is treated similarly. She has raised the standard. But for Lucille, at least at this county club, it's par for the course. I find this inspiring.

As we are finishing our soup, our grilled cheese sandwiches are served.

During our meal, our conversation goes in all different directions. Lucille is curious about my life story. I try to keep to an abridged version but find myself telling her about "Vinnie." She is a John Travolta fan so she has a clear understanding of this little girl's fantasy. I wondered if she had any boy crushes when she was younger. I did not think it appropriate to ask.

Lucille mused, "Very interesting."

Yeah, real fascinating Lucille, my sarcastic wit quietly tells me.

"Can I ask you a question, Lucille?"

"Of course, babe, anything. Or just about anything I guess. Ha-ha"

"Lucille, do you really like getting older?"

"Well, I prefer it to the alternative," she quips while brandishing a crooked impish smile. "As I see it, life, age, time all mean about the same thing. Like cinnamons."

I think she means synonyms but it really doesn't matter.

"Aging is merely a continuation of life and time. And that is a good thing. And anti-aging..."

"What do you think of anti-aging, Lucille?"

"Well, anti-aging would be the opposite, now wouldn't it?"

Oh my, I never looked at it that way. "But, seriously Lucille, are you OK with aging?"

"Babe, I am OK with me. I can do nothing about time passing by. I can do something about whether or not I see value in the time I spend living. Is it an asset or a liability? I choose to see my age as an asset. How can I use all that I know and still can do, to enjoy life? I keep growing and learning and changing. I like that. It's exciting. Each day is a new day. Very exciting!"

I am amazed to hear, although not really surprised, that she still finds such enjoyment in each day. When I first started working I had that enthusiasm. Every day everything was new and exciting. I could not wait to get to work. And then when my daughter was born, I trumped that excitement one-thousand fold. Just sitting on the couch watching my baby daughter do nothing more than take in air, was absolutely thrilling. Everything we did together was an adventure. We had so much fun together. Now, work has changed and my daughter has grown, so I move through each day with less excitement, enthusiasm, and thrills.

Lucille tilts her head to the side and looks directly into my eyes. "Babe, I like being me. Do you like being you?"

What happened? Lucille morphed into Muhammad Ali and hit me in the jaw with a left jab. I bob. I weave. I don't fool Lucille. She knows I am ducking her as I can't respond with a simple affirmation. She nudges my arm, "Watch this."

As if using a piece of chalk to write on an imaginary blackboard, she raises her fork and draws two letters in the air. Down, up, around, and around and then another, down and up again. I visualize two letters, "B U".

"B U?" I say slowly almost slurring the letters.

"Yes, B U— It is time to be you."

"Why did you just use the two letters "B U" instead of writing out the entire words, be you?"

"Simple, it is my contribution to the tweeties."

Did this silver haired old woman make an actual reference to social media users? I purse my lips to hold back my laugh. I don't bother to correct her either. "Oh," I sigh, as if it all makes sense.

The conversation stops for a moment. And then Lucille follows up with a simple thought, "Babe, if you allow yourself to be you, just be yourself, then you would see what an asset you have in being the age that you are. Highlight yourself. Focus on what you have. Show off your talents and the skills you have learned. Be who you really are. I guarantee it will feel good. It is time, babe, to realize you are your best asset."

"I get it Lucille. This is another example of crystallized intelligence in action."

Lucille nods and laughs, "Oh you are so smart, babe."

My, my Lucille, I know I am smart. I want to feel smart, like you do. And I realize the first thing I need to do is to change my perspective about how I see myself, especially how I see myself at this age. If I change my perspective of how I see my age it will impact how I behave and how others react to me.

When I look in the mirror that healthy opinion of myself would be reflected right back at me. If I feel good on the inside, it will come through on the outside. It is a very simple, first step. It's time to make my age my best asset.

We finish our sandwiches and the waitress once again comes to our table. This time, she clears away our empty plates and inquires if we want dessert. Lucille orders a decaf coffee with a Sambuca on the rocks. "Too late in the day for caffeine," Lucille explains. She offers no explanation for ordering the digestif.

My lunch hour has just about expired. I tell Lucille that I have to pass on the dessert as I need to get back to the office. As I am telling her I have to leave, I realize I really do not want to leave. We have spent only one lunch hour together; it simply is not enough time.

"See you for lunch tomorrow, babe?"

I was thrilled Lucille invited me to an encore performance. "Sure, see you tomorrow, Lucille." And then as if I had known her all my life, I rise from my seat, hug and kiss her, and bid her so long.

As I exit the dining area I feel a sense of belonging. My steps are livelier. I smile at the members and staff and some of them actually smile back. I feel good. I can't wait to get back to the office and see how my afternoon plays out.

All the way back to the office, I replay our lunch conversation. I remind myself that I need to change my perspective. I can see Lucille writing in the air and I keep hearing her say, "babe, remember to be yourself—it's time to make your age your best asset."

1st DIAMOND

CHANGE YOUR PERSPECTIVE

2nd DIAMOND

I wake this morning anticipating today's lunch with Lucille. Last night I had an unusually restless sleep, repeatedly tossing one way and turning another. Each time I changed positions I woke up. And each time I woke up I replayed a snippet of yesterday's lunch with Lucille; the tragic loss of her husband, her later-in-life career move, and even the amusing answering machine scenario. All night long I kept seeing people lining up to touch her and how she so generously touched them back.

In spite of my lack of sleep, I feel refreshed and cannot wait to get to the country club. Unfortunately, first I have to get through the morning at work. I arrive on time, turn on my computer, and check off a few prioritized items on my to-do list including responding to several day-old unimportant emails and attending a staff meeting. Thankfully, the morning hours are productive and pass quickly.

Before leaving for the country club, I venture into the restroom to freshen up. I wash my hands, refresh my make-up, and comb my hair. I stare at my reflection in the mirror and remind myself that if I feel good on the inside, it will show on the outside. I am unsure how to change my perspective when it comes to this challenge, as it has always been the other way around—look good, feel good. Now I want it to be—feel good, look good. I remind myself to add "have a long talk with my glabella" to my to-do list and leave for the country club.

I arrive at the country club right before noon. I wasn't thinking I would get there before Lucille, I was just hoping I would not keep her waiting. I know how precious her time is.

I park my car in just about the same spot as always and walk up the path to the clubhouse and into the lobby. The elevator doors are uncharacteristically in a fully opened position. I teasingly convince myself that they have been intentionally left that way in anticipation of my arrival. As soon as I exit the elevator and begin my walk through the dining area, I see Lucille; that same model, sitting at the same table, in the same chair. And this time her photo-op is no less memorable. She is on fire! From the top of her head to the bottom of her toes she is fully adorned in red. Flaming red everything!

Her floppy ruby-red hat could have won first prize at any Kentucky Derby party. And her blouse and skirt are sharply coordinated shades of cardinal red styled to accentuate that winning look. She wears a complementing set of candy-apple red costume jewelry complete with big baubles earrings, or earbobs as Kitty would say, and a matching dangling bracelet. Her scarf, her shoes, and even her pocketbook, that hangs from some gadget clipped to the side of the table, is some shade of the primary color. Her nail polish is also fire engine red.

And there, as a beacon of hope rising from the flames, is the four-diamond brooch perfectly positioned on the left hand side of her blouse right over her heart. Every time I see those diamonds, they make me smile. They are illuminating. And Lucille enhances their light. I know I've said it before, but I have to say it again, I really would like to have my own four-diamond brooch.

As yesterday, the ever-brilliant gems are dwarfed by the radiant smile which guides me through the maze of tables directly to Lucille. Yet, unlike yesterday,

I do not doubt she will remember me. I am certain she knows who I am so I take that one additional confident step and lean over to greet her with a hug and kiss. She returns my wordless message with her welcoming sound. "Hi ya babe, good to see you."

"Good to see you too Lucille, you look very nice...as always."

"All part of it, babe," as she confirms with a wink and nod and no further explanation.

After I take my seat Lucille and I engage in small talk. We both disregard the menus that have been placed on the table and chitchat about the lovely weather and the comfortable room temperature; nothing of any real importance. The usual waitress approaches to explain the daily specials. Like Lucille, I give her my full attention as she begins to recite today's specials. "Our special entrée today is penne pasta with..."

"Oh that's wonderful. That will hit the spot," Lucille cuts her off sounding fully satisfied even before she or I have the opportunity to hear what it comes with or if there are any other specials of equal or lesser value. Lucille is content. "I will have the penne pasta.

You can't beat a good dish of macaroni. Make it with marinara sauce and make it al dente. That comes with a side salad, right?"

"Yes, that is correct. Balsamic vinaigrette house dressing OK?"

"Sure, house dressing is fine."

I save the waitress from having to ask for my order, "Sounds good to me. I will have the exact same."

Lucille does not provide the waitress with an opportunity to inquire about our drink order. Instead, Lucille tells her she will have a glass of Chianti with her lunch. I would love to join her, but once again, I have to get back to work, so once again I order iced tea—unsweetened of course.

As the waitress removes the menus from the table and walks toward the kitchen, Lucille calls out to her to "remember to bring the salad after the pasta, not before."

"Got it, Lucille," the server yells back.

I have never heard of such a sequence of food, pasta before salad instead of salad before pasta, but my newly-appointed mentor is schooling me in many things, including Italian culinary customs. I can't wait to try it.

Just like yesterday, when the drink order is served, Lucille raises her glass to mine and without skipping a beat, toasts, "Salute, Cent'anni." This time I have more of an ear for the foreign words and a better idea of what I am talking about. "Cent'anni, Lucille." We clink glasses and I watch as she savors her first sip of red wine. I take a sip of my iced tea and realize it needs sweetener.

"So, how have you been?" Lucille opens the conversation.

"Pretty good," I say, thinking I just saw you twenty four hours ago.

"How have you been?"

Lucille laughs, "I have been just fine, babe. Bonanza was a repeat." We share our inside joke, knowing full well the show has been off the air for thirty years.

I begin to tell Lucille how I was starting to change my perspective about this time in my life.

She is leaning forward as if she is extremely interested in everything I have to say. I tell her that in our weekly staff meeting this morning when we were discussing work issues and trying to problem solve, I heard myself using such phrases as "what if we looked at it a different way and what happens if we change our perspective?"

"Is that what you would usually bring to the meeting?"

"Not really. As a rule I refrain from adding any opinion and roll my eyes about all the stuff that goes on."

"So how's that work for you?'

"The eye rolling?"

"No, babe, I have a pretty good idea of how effective eye rolling can be in a meeting."

"Oh yeah...well, for starters I felt like I had something to contribute."

"And then what happened."

"Well, when it came to this one item on the agenda I suggested that we sit down and talk about it with the people and really try to understand what is going on from their perspective and how we can fix it."

"That's exciting. And what was happening in the room when you were speaking."

"Hum, let me think." I mentally replay what went down in the meeting and report to Lucille, "One manager, who I could barely see, not because she is a size zero, but because she was sitting on the same side of the conference table as me but at the other end, leaned way in over the table to get my attention and asked, 'Do you think you can reach out and bring those people together to get a real sense of what is going on and figure out where we go from here? Do you think you can get a team together to compile a report and make a presentation to the C-suite to help them make the final decision? Can you do that?' "

"So what did you answer when she asked, can you do that?"

"I responded without hesitation, 'Sure. I can do that.' I mean, I know how to talk to people and build relationships; listen to their viewpoints. I can problem solve. I can identify priorities. I can work with people to uncover solutions. I can do all that."

"What about the presentation part of it? Can you do that, too?"

"Actually, I turned to my tech-savvy MBA twins and asked them if they would be willing to help with the multi-media aspect of the presentation."

"What did they say?"

"The MBA twins jumped on the invitation with the same enthusiasm of having found out they just won tickets to Disneyworld, 'Sure, that will be fun.'"

"So how did you feel?"

"Well, I definitely did not feel left out."

Lucille winks at me. "Very, very exciting."

"Come to think of it, it was exciting."

"Did you feel smart?"

I nod my head up and down to indicate yes and mutter, "Yeah, but now I have a lot more work to do."

"Now you have an opportunity to showcase your talents and play to your strengths," Lucille snaps back.

"There you go, Lucille, a classic change of perspective."

Lucille shakes her head in agreement.

"And then you know what else I did Lucille?"

"I can't wait to hear, babe. Tell me, tell me, babe," Lucille says with a youthful enthusiasm.

And then I tell Lucille what happened with the CIO whose face is glued to his mobile computer and who I don't think really knows I exist so I ignore him right back.

"Well Lucille, what I did was when he walked by my cubicle, I got up and walked over to him and called him by his first name and asked him if I could have five minutes of his time."

"And..."

"He actually raised his head and looked at me. And then he said, 'What's up?' "

"And..."

"And then I told him that I couldn't figure out how to use one of the new computer applications."

"And..."

"And he showed me."

"And..."

"And I understood how to do it."

"And..."

"And...he is very nice. He has lovely eyes. And he really is smart. I told him that, not the eye thing, just that he was very helpful and that I appreciated him taking the time to help me."

"And..."

"And then he flashed a never-before-seen smile and said, 'No prob.' And if I ever get stuck again, I am to 'Just give a holler.' That's it."

"That is absolutely fascinating."

"Yeah, I think so too. It really was easy."

"Babe, changing your perspective will open you up to many other things. I once heard that if we change the way we look at things, the things we look at change," she says obviously to encourage me.

It is very difficult not to agree with Lucille. Everything she says makes sense, fundamental sense. I think they call it common sense only it really isn't too common these days. How does she do that?

"You know, Lucille, I am going to work on changing my perspective about how I see myself at this stage in my life. Sometimes, though, especially when I look in the mirror...well you know...I just don't look like I used to"

"Good thing, eh?"

What? Are you kidding me? It takes every ounce of self-control not to yell back, IT SUCKS! Instead, I just shake my head and with clenched teeth and a piercing look firmly state, "I hate how I look these days. I used to have smooth skin and now it is blotchy. I used to have silky hair and now it is multi-color with wiry gray strands running rampant. I used to be attractive and now I don't think I am."

Lucille does not totally dismiss my rant. She stays true to form, waits until I ease up a bit and then takes her turn. "You know, babe, every other Saturday morning, my children would sit on the front porch of the house and wait for me to return from the beauty parlor. They wanted to see what color my hair would be—sometimes it was blonde, sometimes red, and one time even pink. I dyed my hair for so many years that I, too, was not quite sure what color my hair was. But this one day, I must have been about your age, I told my beautician that I no longer wanted to color my hair. I told her I was done covering up. I wanted to get back to my roots, so to speak. And my roots were gray"

"I bet your hairdresser was not too pleased with that decision."

"Well, she sure was quite surprised. And more importantly she was totally supportive." Lucille points to a woman in the restaurant who was her hairdresser at the time.

I give a quick glance in the direction of the other woman and then return to question Lucille. "Why did you decide to expose your gray hair?"

"More than deciding to expose my gray hair was my decision to let go of the past. I was moving on. My skin was changing, my body was changing, and most importantly, I was changing. So why continue to hold on to something that I could not?"

"Did it make you feel old when you unmasked your gray hair?"

"Actually...quite the opposite. I felt in control. And that was exhilarating, youthful and fun."

"You freed yourself from the shackles of peroxide!" I declare triumphantly.

"You're funny. Practicing that 'change your perspective' concept, eh? You are correct, what I did was look at it differently and let go of the past. I moved forward and I was proud of myself. Plain and simple."

Lucille begins to tell me about her daughter's high school friend. Lucille described her as a very tall, slender girl with big brown eyes and long flowing black hair.

"In high school, she reminded me of Cher. She was tall and thin and had long, silky dark hair that almost reached her waist. Every once in a while she would jerk her neck so her hair would flip over her shoulder. Just like Cher. You know Sonny and Cher right? Very pretty girl."

Yes, Lucille, I know Sonny and Cher and I get the picture.

Lucille goes on to say that several years ago her daughter celebrated a high school reunion and her "Cher-friend" was in town so she stopped by the house.

"You know, babe, I am always glad to see people I know and I was so surprised to see "Cher.""

"Well, how did she look? Did she still look like Cher?"

I take a sip of my iced tea. Lucille takes a sip of her wine and declares, "She looked more like Elvira!"

I choke with laughter and Lucille is right behind me with a cackle. And then Lucille clarifies that she meant no disrespect to Cher or Elvira. "It is just that in the case of my daughter's friend, she is trying to hold onto the past. We change, and that is OK, in fact it is a good thing."

"I have to admit, Lucille, I would be so afraid to let myself go gray."

"What is there to be afraid of?"

I remain silent for a moment to mull Lucille's question and add a few of my own. What am I afraid of? Will the gray hair make me look older? Lucille looks beautiful and stunning. Aren't gray haired women bitchy? Lucille surely isn't a bitch. Isn't our culture obsessed with hiding the gray and holding on to the same look we have had since we were in high school? Lucille doesn't fear change. She actually embraces it and finds it exhilarating.

"Come to think of it Lucille, I'm really not sure."

"What if you looked at it this way—just let yourself go—let yourself be you. Focus on self-content and who you are now."

Ah, if I could just give myself permission and let go. As I am digesting Lucille's words, our pasta is served. Penne pasta with RED marinara sauce. She didn't really choose this entrée because it matched her outfit, did she?

Like yesterday, and with no forewarning, Lucille reaches into her pocketbook and pulls out a bib for me to fasten around her neck. Only today, you guessed it, the bib is red. And it is red sateen! And it matches her outfit to a tee. No big surprise. I rise from my seat, fasten the bib with the Velcro strip, sit back down in my chair and start eating.

The luncheon conversation is interesting and, at times, silly. Lucille is such a character! Her sense of humor is definitely one of her finer points. She tells me about the "little old ladies" in a senior club she belongs to who talk only of the good old days and their aches and pains.

I was amused by her use of the phrase "little old ladies" and I ask her point blank, "Lucille, how old are you?"

"Babe, you never ask a lady how old she is. You know that."

And then she takes a swig of wine and proudly declares, "I am like this well aged Chianti, I am ninety-two."

Holy Mackerel! I thought she was eighty or eighty-two the most. What makes her appear so youthful? Is it her smile, the way she carries herself, her playfulness, her candidness or her willingness to learn and explore new things? What the hell is it? Whatever it is she needs to bottle it and hit the QVC airways because it is definitely working for this nonagenarian.

"Lucille, I think letting go of the past is a difficult thing to do."

"Yes, I guess it is."

And then for one of the first times, Lucille looks pensive and remains quiet.

She takes a small forkful of pasta, adds some chopped hot red pepper directly onto the bite-sized portion and eats it.

After swallowing what must have been a very spicy mouthful, she continues to hold onto her fork in one hand and uses her other hand to mindlessly coax more red pepper from its shaker onto her entire bowl of pasta. I don't think she is paying too much attention to what she is doing with the spice. Instead, she seems to be more focused on relating a story for my benefit. "Remember I told you I had a daughter?"

"Yes, I remember."

"Well, when my husband was in the hospital and his days to live could be counted on one hand, the hospital let me sneak the kids in to see their dad in his room. I'm unsure if you remember but in those days, children were not allowed in hospitals. Anyway, I am not too sure if they really understood what was going on. But after the visit, when we were walking to the car in the parking lot, I looked up and saw my husband standing at his room window waving. If I remember correctly, he was on the fifth floor. I told the kids to turn around and look up at dad and wave to him. All three did exactly as I asked."

I put my fork down, cut short my chewing and swallow my pasta almost whole because I really want to show Lucille she has my undivided attention. She goes on to tell me that about twenty years after that day, she and her daughter were having martinis together, as they did from time to time, at one of the local bars and the hospital incident came up in their conversation.

"My daughter is a good woman. Like a lot of kids she had her struggles, especially with me," she openly admits. "As she got older, I always thought that she had something bothering her or haunting her, so to speak, that held her back a bit and I never really understood what that was all about. And then this one day after our second martini, my daughter said she had a confession. I was thinking, oh boy, I am going to be a grandmother." She pauses momentarily and seems to be carefully considering the best way to tell me what it is she wants me to know.

Lucille's voice softens as she relates what her daughter admitted, "Mom," she said, "I didn't see daddy in the window when I looked up."

Lucille is sad. I cannot only hear it in her voice, I can see it as well. Her posture dips, her shoulders drop, and her head droops, making her appear smaller and weaker. She releases a deep sigh which propels her to continue. "You know babe, at that very moment I felt so bad for my daughter. I could sense the pain of guilt she had been carrying. I realized she carried this unnecessary sense of failure with her for so long and she had talked herself into feeling like she was a disappointment. I looked at her and said, 'Sweetheart, you were only four years old, you were not expected to find the one window in the sea of windows. You may not have seen your daddy but your daddy sure saw you.'"

Again, Lucille sounds melancholy. And then she bounces right back with, "And as soon as my daughter accepted that perspective and let go of that piece of her past, I could see a change in her."

"Like how?" I really want to know.

"A level of peacefulness came over her. She got lighter. She smiled more. She laughed more. She changed careers and opened her own business. She met a wonderful man—a sense of youthfulness came over her. She got married—had three children—all that good stuff."

As Lucille is telling me about how "light" her daughter became when she let go of her burdensome past, Lucille seems "lighter," too. She rearranges herself in her chair, pulling her shoulders back and raising her head. Once again, she is sitting tall. She takes a hearty bite of her pasta and seems totally oblivious to the fact that it is overly saturated with spicy crushed red pepper.

When Lucille ends her story, I start to think of all those things that have happened to me over the years and how some of them still make me feel bad about myself. I do carry a lot of what others have said to me, done to me, and the unrealistic image of what I am supposed to be—failed relationships, past mistakes, workplace blow-ups, body image concerns and the like. So much proverbial baggage.

Lucille asks, "Babe, how much do you think your fork weighs?"

I consider myself a quick learner and I know to simply go with Lucille, so I respond without much thought.

"Not much, a couple of ounces, maybe."

"Yes, it really doesn't amount to much, does it?"

"No, not really."

"What do you think would happen if you held onto the same fork for an hour?"

"Besides being bored, I guess I would feel quite uncomfortable."

"What do you think would happen if you held onto the same fork for a day?"

"I guess it would feel really, really uncomfortable and it would seem much heavier than a few ounces. My fingers would get cramped I am sure."

"How about a week, a month, a year, many years?"

I interrupt Lucille, "OK, I get it. I get it"

"Your hands might look like mine," as she shows me her hands and releases a bit of self-deprecating humor, "Beauties aren't they?"

When Lucille displays her hands, I see they are bony and bent, obviously full of arthritis. I'm shocked. I never noticed their frailty before.

"Now, as time goes on, you may pick up other burdens." She hands me my iced tea, the red pepper shaker, and a spoon. "If you had to hold on to all those things for a period of time how do you think you would feel?"

"Well, if things keep piling on I would feel weak, tired, and probably achy. Eventually I would be unable to keep up with the load."

"What do you think would happen if good things, like opportunity or really colorful jewelry, ha ha, came your way? How would you be able to grab the good?"

I pause for a second, "Well, if my hands are full and I am tired and weak, I would not have the option or strength to grab hold of anything, including jewelry. Ha, ha. "

"You bet. That is what holding on to those things from your past does to you. Makes you tired, achy and actually weakens you. You can't keep up or grab hold. Makes you feel old and heavy."

"That would stress me out."

"Yes it does stress us out. And the stress shows in our looks, how we act, how we feel and of course, how we feel about ourselves."

As Lucille finishes her statement, I replay all my losses, worries, and failures. I think of them, I see them, I hear them, and I usually relive them over and over again in one way or another just about every day. I judge myself and I judge others. What would happen if I moved on from them and just left them there in the past, where they belonged? I sure would feel a lot lighter! Is this what Lucille is talking about? Move on, it's over. What was in the past is in the past. What is now is new and exciting.

By now, both Lucille and I have had our fill of the pasta and move our dishes aside. Right on cue, the waitress brings our salads. I have never eaten my salad after my pasta before. It is like a vegetable dessert! How cool is that!

While we gnaw on the mixture of leafy greens, a diverse entourage of people, some dressed in professional business attire, others in designer-logoed golf apparel and even others with poorly coordinated stretch-waist pants and shirt-like jackets, stop by our table. Each person hugs and kisses Lucille. Lucille introduces me over and over again. One of the women she is anxious for me to meet is her former hairdresser—her "beautician friend" as she calls her. The beautician friend has beautiful gray hair, too, and also dons a four-diamond brooch, albeit not as bold as

Lucille's. All of a sudden the country club looks like a sorority house with a host of women sporting smaller replicas of the four-diamond brooch being drawn to Lucille to pay their respects. Lucille is just sitting there and yet powerfully attracting people. Her magnetic field expands beyond the restaurant into the bar area and even the lobby. It is absolutely amazing. No one else does the same.

When Lucille and I are alone again, I confide to her that I do hang on to things that have gone on before. She smiles and nods and tells me that she could tell that I carry some deep burdens with me. "It is not that unusual for people, especially women to do that."

"I agree with you Lucille. Many of us are constantly under a lot of pressure making it rather difficult to simply let go and just be ourselves."

"Did you know diamonds are formed under extreme pressure?"

I have to admit to Lucille that the only things I know about diamonds are that they are beautiful and out of my price range. She shrugs her shoulders as if to say, "maybe, maybe not" and then explains to me that diamonds are formed deep within the earth, under very hot temperatures and with a lot of pressure. It is not until they rise to the top of the earth's surface and expose themselves that we are able to share in their own beauty.

Lucille casually comments, "I guess diamonds are like people. They need to let go of their past so they can just be the magnificent gem they are meant to be. That way they can enjoy this time in their existence and shine for everyone to see."

As I mumble under my breath, "diamonds are just so beautiful," I hear Lucille mumble as well as if she is speaking only to her forkful of romaine lettuce, "Diamonds are billions of years old. How 'bout that for age."

I could have stayed another hour or two with Lucille if my schedule would have allowed. Instead, I finish my "dessert" and let Lucille know I need to get back to the office as I have a to-do list I need to tackle.

"No problem. I understand. Do you have a balloon?"

"Ah...what? A balloon, no not on me," I remark while thinking what a strange thing to ask. No one carries balloons with them.

"Well, pick up a balloon at the discount store after you leave the club."

I now know for a fact that Lucille uses a really smooth technique to segue into having me do something that I would not normally do. Her actions border on entrapment. The longer I am in her company, the more I am "on to her" so I ask a straightforward question. "What for?"

"To help you."

"Excuse me? Help me do what?"

"Free yourself from the shackles of whatever! Help you let go of the past, of course. Help you rid yourself of anything that is burdensome and weighing you down."

I still do not understand how a balloon will help me rid myself of self-imposed burdens and yet I am confident Lucille knows. I remain in my seat and listen closely.

"Here is what I want you to do when you go home tonight. Blow up a balloon. Take a marker. Oh yeah, remember to pick up a marker at the discount store too. You will need one. Now, after you blow up the balloon, make a knot in it. Stare at the balloon and think about all those things from your past; people, phrases, events—whatever—that still bother you. Take your time and think really hard. Write them on the balloon, one at a time. Write slowly and take a good hard look at what you've written. This is very important. Don't forget, don't forget, take your time and think," she persuasively reiterates to ensure my compliance.

Once I respond with an obedient, "OK," Lucille finishes her instructions. "And then...say good bye, adios or ciao, and stick a pin in the balloon, pop that damn windbag, and send those burdens into smithereens!"

I let out a roar as I visualize myself going through the motions and realize where she is going with the exercise. "I sure as hell would not be able to put the balloon back together now would I?"

"You are so smart, babe. You are right. The balloon and everything you wrote on it would be splintered into tiny bits and absolutely worthless to you."

"Lucille, I think I may need a bag of balloons."

"You are funny, babe."

With that kind thought, I hug and kiss Lucille and bid her so long. As I make my exit, Lucille, as she did yesterday, proposes we meet again tomorrow for lunch. And as yesterday, I accept with sincere appreciation for her invitation.

Before I leave the club I check the time on my cell phone. I am pleased to see I have just enough time to stop by the discount store to buy a balloon—a bag of balloons. And I won't forget the marker. This is going to be fun!

Annarose Ingarra-Milch

2nd DIAMOND

LET GO OF THE PAST

3rd DIAMOND

The shrill pitch of my alarm clock awakens me. Last night's sleep was interrupted with balloons bursting; pop, pop, pop, one right after another like fireworks. Blow it up, mark it up, bust it up. Pop! Pop! Pop! I can't get the sound out of my head. I can't get Lucille out of my head either. I am anxious to get to the country club and have lunch with Lucille.

Changing my perspective and letting go of the past are indeed exercises for me. Admittedly, when I put Lucille's lessons into action and look at my age as an asset while moving on from what has gone on before in my life that weighs me down, I really do notice significant changes.

I am more energetic and lively. My mind seems sharper. This morning when I looked in the mirror I swore that image reflected back at me. I was even able to crack a smile knowing full well that the rutted glabella highway running down the center of my face continues to be in need of re-tarring.

On top of how I see myself, I think others "see" me differently. For example, yesterday when I returned to the office after lunch, I was speaking with Ms. MBA, the other Ms. MBA, and Margie about the project the four of us are supposedly working on together. We ran into each other in the break room. Margie and I had just finished our coffee. We were going out. They were coming in.

I nudged Margie to signal her to stop from walking out of the room. I interrupted the Ms. MBAs before they could get involved in preparing their nonfat, sugar-free, skinny latte, with a simple, "Hey, you guys have a minute?"

In unison I heard, "What's up?" The MBA twins were standing next to each other shoulder to shoulder, facing Margie and me, who were also shoulder to shoulder, and facing them. If I were to measure the distance between the couples I would say that Margie and I were standing a comfortable social distance of about five feet away from the MBA couple; easy enough to hear and see each other, too far to touch each other. Each twin had her hands in front of her, down by her waist, with thumbs idle on her megaG cell phone keypad. Margie's arms were folded and tightly tucked in front of her across her breastbone, creating a convenient shelf for her well-endowed boobs. My hands were hanging comfortably at my sides.

I opened the conversation with the fact that our joint project deadline was approaching. The blonde MBA quickly suggested some ideas and prefaced each one with "How about we try this?" The brunette MBA, just as quickly, rattled off other options usually beginning with "I have an idea." Personally, I don't think either one of them was listening to what the other one was saying. However, I found myself listening, or at least trying to listen, to both of them.

Margie was locked and loaded and gunning for bear. With double barrels pointed at the twins, Margie's dismissive voice came across loud and clear. Following each of their recommendations she would shoot back, opening each of her statements with "Yes, but I don't think that we should" or "No that won't work." One time she even resorted to "Been there, done that." No kidding, it was the only time she opened up her posture so she could reload her shotgun.

While something like a conversation was transpiring, I felt a bit removed as if I was watching an artificial scenario that didn't include me, but in reality I knew it did. My head moved back and forth as I tried to give attention to everyone on the firing range. I moved out of my squared-off position to a more rounded one which inadvertently reduced the social distance and allowed for better eye contact between the four of us. And then, as if on cue everyone shifted just slightly and we were standing in a circle.

Ms. MBA's eyes, which are brown like her hair which I noticed for the first time, made contact with mine. Instead of looking at me, however, I felt her looking "to" me. "So what do you think?" In all the time we have been working together, neither one of the twins ever uttered those five words to me. I was taken aback by her apparent deference. And then I heard myself respond with an appropriate dose of self-confidence, "Well, I am hearing a lot of good ideas, from each of you. After you guys are done with your break, let's all go into the conference room and see if we can collaborate on how to proceed." And with that, the quartet nodded in agreement. I slapped myself on the back, figuratively, of course, and heard a congratulatory inner voice (or maybe it was Lucille's voice), "way to go, babe!"

I am beginning to see Lucille's impact on me not only in work situations but at home as well. My daughter called last evening. Since her teen years and her father leaving, we seem to live in a series of disagreements. For example, I think every boyfriend she dates is a loser, and she thinks they are all winners. I think her tattoos are graffiti, she thinks they're art. Piercing my earlobes is enough, piercing every other part of her body is still not enough.

And then, of course, there is her perpetual sniveling. Her telephonic ranting monologues make me glad I've upgraded my cell phone plan to unlimited anytime minutes. While she goes on and on, I take the opportunity to celebrate my business acumen. I pause and recall my balloon exercise and that I had "exploded' my mother/daughter angst. Nevertheless it is still a challenge for me to keep from growing angry and snapping "I am tired of hearing you whine little girl." I ask myself, how would Lucille handle this? She would probably say something like, "Whine? Did you say whine? I prefer my wine to be red and dry."

A picture of a sassy Lucille flashes into my head and it amuses me. I remember how she deescalated the answering machine debacle and figure I have to do likewise with my twenty-two year old daughter. This time I think before I speak to ensure my voice comes across with believable concern, "I hear ya. How about we meet for dinner tomorrow and talk more. My treat. You choose the place." And with that, the complaining ends. "Sure. Sounds good. Talk more then. There is a new gluten-free restaurant we can try."

"Great, let's do it!" I didn't have the heart to tell her I love gluten.

She sounded thrilled with my spontaneity and liveliness. Now that was definitely a change. And again I hear a voice saying "way to go, babe!" Who is that? Lucille? Jiminy Cricket? Or me?

It is approaching lunchtime and I am getting anxious to leave the office. I go into the ladies room and perform my usual primping ritual. I see the gray hair screaming from my temples and today I opt not to silence it. I will test the waters and pull my hair back to expose rather than hide the salt. I have to admit, I am not too sure about this move.

When I arrive at the country club I park my car in my usual spot. I enter the clubhouse and ride the elevator up one flight to the dining area as I have done each day this week. I cannot wait to tell Lucille about her influence on me—how I see myself and how I have started investing in my best asset—me!

Just as yesterday and the day before that and every day I have ever seen Lucille she is poised at her table in the dining room. Today it is a black and white day. From head to toe everything she wears, is black or white. Not a slight gray, not an off-white, only pure diametrically opposing, good old black and white.

Every stitch of clothing, blouse, slacks, jacket, shoes and every single accessory, scarf, pocketbook, jewelry, hat, is either black or white. She looks so powerful in the coordinated and contrasting outfit. And along with that strong sense of self is a touch of easiness.

Lucille's hat, which resembles Charlie Chaplin's bowler with a slightly larger brim, is only half there! It reminds me of when I made cookies last year at holiday time. After I rolled out the dough I used my circular cookie cutter to sculpt half-dollar sized round cookies. It is as if the milliner made a pattern from the remaining devil's food, holey sheet of dough and shaped it into Lucille's black felt hat.

It is a remarkable piece of creativity and like nothing I have ever seen before! Only Lucille can get away with wearing a hat that others may reserve for Halloween and have it look so stylish and chic. I bet Lucille wears it because she knows it creates another opportunity to show off her beautiful, white hair through the holes and add one more black and white accessory. Or maybe it's just fun!

If I have to make a quick judgment, I deem Lucille to be a jewelry junkie. She seems to have so many different pieces, colors and themes of jewelry. In our conversations she has admitted that buying costume jewelry is exhilarating and worn correctly, ties the outfit together. Today, Lucille's jewelry is tying in masterfully. Her black and white, isosceles triangle-shaped, dangling, clip-on plastic earrings complement, without fully matching, her black and white choker necklace which is in the shape of a bowtie. On her wrist is a two-inch wide band, black and white bracelet. And there, for all to see, right alongside her jacket lapel in the same place over her heart, is the four-diamond brooch, shining brightly and exuding a sense of power that perfectly aligns with the black and white fully contrasting and yet fully coordinated outfit.

Today, as every day I have had the pleasure to lunch with Lucille, she looks like a model. She always looks as manicured as the golf course right behind her. If this were a photo shoot the only thing that would change is the color of her outfits and her carefully selected props.

My eyes quickly shift to her perpetual grin which she uses to light the path to my seat. Before I take my usual seat at the table, I go around to her side of the table to hug and kiss her. And as usual she greets me as if she has not seen me in years. "Hi ya babe, good to see ya!"

It is very difficult to respond to Lucille other than with similar enthusiasm and warm emotion, "Hi ya Lucille, it is so good to see you too!"

I am confident Lucille senses my eagerness to tell her what is going on in my life and how I am beginning to enjoy, if that is the proper word, my age.

Without skipping a beat, Lucille leans into me and opens the discussion, "So tell me all about it, babe."

And the spigot opens! I just have to tell Lucille how I was seeing myself and how others were reacting to me. I was moving off the "I feel stupid, I feel ugly, I feel old" mantras and hearing more of "I know this, I am sharp, I can do this."

I tell her about the impromptu meeting with Margie and the twins. I relay how Margie shot down just about every suggestion the twins offered.

Lucille asked, "What do you think that was all about?"

"I think Margie has a tough time letting go of the past and opening herself up to new ideas to move forward. I can definitely relate."

Lucille grabs for her wallet, pulls out a crinkled ten dollar bill and shoves it into my palm.

"What's this for?" You know come to think of it, no money is ever exchanged in this establishment. People just sign for everything.

"Babe, take the sawbuck and pick up a case of balloons for Margie, my compliments." We laugh together. I slip the money back into the pocket of her black jacket.

When I tell her how the MBA twins were talking but it seemed that neither one was listening she says,

"They sound ill. My guess is they have been stricken with Worsitis."

"Worsitis. Is that an actual disease? I have never heard of it."

"Oh, yes, it is a horrible disease."

"Is it contagious?" I ask, half-sensing she is pulling my leg. The other half of me toys with the slightest possibility that given both her husband and son were doctors, medical knowledge may be inherited.

"Highly," Lucille says convincingly.

"Worsitis is when one person says something like, 'I have this serious aching pain, I can hardly move and I am close to death.' And the other person says, 'Oh that's nothing, I have an even worse serious aching pain, I really can't move and I may die sooner.' "

"Very funny, you almost had me, Lucille."

"Anyone of any age can suffer from this ugly disease. When you stop listening to another person, the disease can creep into your bones. And people will shy away from you. You will no longer be attractive to them and probably not to yourself as well."

"You know Lucille, come to think of it, I don't know if the twins were aware of Margie's biting remarks."

"Maybe, maybe not. But if someone treated you the same way, would you feel the sting? How many times would you go back, how close would you get to someone if you knew you'd get stung each time?"

Lucille takes a breath and then commends me, "Babe, I am glad you have not been afflicted nor chosen to be a carrier."

Feeling somewhat ashamed to admit that I previously may have been infected, I clear my throat and report to Lucille, "I am glad, too."

"Babe, now that is beautiful," Lucille affirms.

After Lucille punctuates her declaration, she stays silent. My guess is she wants to give me time to wrap my head around a new version and real meaning of attractiveness and beauty.

Lucille is obviously quite pleased with me and how I am taking action on what she has been sharing with me. She pats my hand, "Ah, Grasshopper, you smart, attractive woman."

You know, that was the first time anyone has ever said that to me. And for sure, I am beginning to believe it. It is also the first time anyone has referred to me as "grasshopper." Actually I am learning so much from Lucille, I really am beginning to identify with Kwai Chang Caine from the old television series, *Kung Fu.*

When the conversation lulls, the waitress approaches our table. She has no menus with her. Instead she looks directly at Lucille and says, as if broadcasting a news flash, "Today the chef is offering one of your favorite dishes Lucille, steak tartare." Lucille smiles broadly, "Oh how wonderful! What a surprise. Will you join me babe?"

I have come very far with Lucille over the past few days. But eating raw, ground beef topped with a raw egg yolk is stretching my limits. And then without hesitation I hear myself, "What the hell, I will try it." Oh my, am I turning into a risk-taker? I jokingly ask myself.

Lucille orders a Jack Daniel's on the rocks with a splash and wedge, as she did on our first lunch date. Today, I am seriously thinking that I will need something with a kick to ensure I will be able to digest the culinary delicacy I ordered. Unfortunately, I have another few hours of work ahead so I do not indulge.

The waitress makes eye contact with me and confirms, "Iced tea, unsweetened, right?" "Yes, thank you." Having her remember my drink helps me understand why her job title is "hospitality expert." After all, I am not a card-carrying member of the country club. I am, however, having lunch with Lucille.

As soon as the waitress leaves our table, I refocus our conversation. I tell Lucille how I now understand that it is through my years of living that I have gained an enormous amount of knowledge and know-how. I even refer to myself as a crystallized intelligent woman. I know this pleases her.

And then our drinks are served. I pick up my glass and before Lucille can get the words out, I take the lead and nobly state, "Salute Cent'anni."

Again, Lucille looks pleased, and responds, "Salute Cent'anni babe, well said."

We each take a sip of our drinks. Lucille puts her glass down and touches my hand as she has done so many times. This time she rhythmically pats—one, two, three times. Her gesture is similar to tapping someone on the shoulder so they will turn around and take notice.

"OK...so what's the plan?"

"What? Plan for what?"

"For you, of course. What are you going to do?"

She says it as if I should know what she is talking about.

"I don't know what you are talking about," pulling my hand away from hers.

My celebratory tone changes to annoyance. Lucille presses me. "I hope you are not thinking you are done," she says with what I interpret as possible disappointment.

I respond with obvious disappointment. "I'm confused. What is it that I have not done? What is it that I am supposed to be doing? Lucille, what else do I need to do for heaven's sake? I have done everything that you have taught me, isn't that enough? I am working on changing my perspective and letting go of the past so I see myself and my intelligence and looks differently. I am working on recognizing my best asset. What else do you want me to do?"

As the words roll off my lips, I am disgusted with my words and actions. I scold myself—YOU JERK! YOU IDIOT!—What is your problem? If you don't know the answer just tell her you don't know. There is no need to send off a nasty verbal email.

Lucille remains quiet as if the screaming going on in my head is deafening to her as well. I am sure she senses that I am feeling ashamed for snapping as I did, especially coming on the heels of my braggadocio. We sit in silence for a minute or two, although it feels like an hour. I am not comfortable at all. I am wondering if Lucille feels equally uncomfortable.

With my eyes fixed downward in a stare on the crisp, white linen tablecloth, I rely on my peripheral vision to reach out and touch Lucille's hand, as she has done to me many times. I choke back my tears and apologetically whisper, "I am so very sorry. What I did was wrong, I should not have snapped at you. If I hurt you, please forgive me."

I can feel Lucille's eyes resting on my face. And I sense no daggers coming from them. Slowly I raise my head and look at Lucille. She is indeed looking straight at me. And she is indeed not showing any anger towards me. Instead, she cracks a half-smile, nods, and winks. Using a soft tone she says, "Babe, you are a good person. What I think of you matters to you. I know that. I know that is important to you. We all care about what other people think about us. And now I see and feel with your touch that what matters to you even more is what you think of you. What you think of you far outweighs what others think of you. Remember— always—character above reputation—always. That builds the powerful woman—the self-confident, self-controlled, self-aware woman. I love you, babe, and you need to feel the same about yourself."

Awkward silence returns. I cannot say another word without weeping so I remain quiet. Then, I imitate my mentor. I look straight at her, smile, nod, and wink. Lesson learned. No more needs to be said.

I am amazed how quickly Lucille forgives me and moves on. And at the same time I am so proud of myself for quickly regaining my composure and returning our focus to the original conversation.

Pulling a tissue from my pocket, I blow my nose and recap, "OK, so where were we before I rudely interrupted us?" We chuckle. "You asked me what the plan is for me?"

I take a deep breath with one last sniffle and shamelessly confess, "I have no plan. I have not even thought about having a plan."

Lucille takes a sip of Jack and returns the glass to its rightful place on the table without releasing it from her grip. "I am really not too surprised. Not many of the people I know have one. They just get up each day and put one foot in front of the other. I guess that is one way to do it. Get less bang for your buck that way, I think, anyway."

"So how do I get more bang for my buck?" I ask figuring her answer should be a real whopper.

"Simple. Take control of your future."

"Simple you say. I can't do that. No one can. How can I control my future?"

Lucille, with her glass already in hand, takes another sip of Jack. I figure a story is right behind her swallow, as usual. And I am right.

"Several months after my husband died and I regained my composure to a degree, a large enough degree to function outside the house anyway, I was playing in a softball game at a summer cook-out with friends and family."

"Whoa, whoa! You used to play softball?"

"Sure did. At that time in my life, I only pitched. I was a designated pitcher, you could say. I had a mitt, spikes, and a uniform. Well, actually I wore five-inch spike heels with matching short shorts and cap of course. I actually pitched well, but I looked even better!" Just visualizing the outfit causes both of us to laugh.

With the enthusiasm of a baseball broadcaster delivering the play by play, she continues. "So it's the bottom of the last inning. We are down by one run. We have our final at bat. Our best hitters are in the fourth and fifth slots in the lineup. Things are getting tense. As I have my eyes fixed on the baseball diamond, I hear our panicking self-appointed captain shout over and over, 'What's the game plan? What's the game plan?' "

Lucille pauses, causing me to anxiously ask, "So, so, so...what was the plan?"

Lucille looks at me, shakes her head from side to side, "Not important. Follow me here."

I am a big fan of the sport and given the situation on the field at Lucille's game, I am anxious to hear how it plays out. Instead, when Lucille says it is not important, I immediately shift my concentration to what she is trying to tell me.

There is always a reason Lucille tells me a story. She is either sharing information, trying to persuade me, or simply being entertaining. I have come to the conclusion that regardless of her delivery mode she is simply trying to teach me something. And in this scenario it probably isn't fundamental baseball.

So I sit back and assure her, "OK, I have my head in the game. I am following you, coach."

Lucille spars right back, "Touché."

And then she goes on to tell me that when she got home that evening after the picnic she kept revisiting the baseball diamond and hearing the question, "What is the game plan? What is the game plan?" It was then she realized that she really didn't have a plan. She was just putting one foot in front of the other. Given her situation it was probably commendable she was even capable of doing that. Yet, she realized that to be really successful, to win, she needed to develop a game plan. So she wrote down her priorities and imagined how she was going to ensure that she focused on those priorities. It was no surprise that her children were her three major priorities, along with herself.

From there, she explained how she saw the future play out. She visualized her kids being healthy, happy, and successful adults and she saw herself living comfortably surrounded by friends and family. She worked back from that vision and determined what she would have to do to make it all happen. She designed her personal game plan, a step by step action plan, as we say at work, which would ensure her and her children's successful future.

I tell Lucille that at work we write goal plans all the time. In fact, I remind her that my team is working on a plan right now. But then I confess that in my "real life," so to speak, I do not even think to write goals.

Lucille picks up on the discrepancy, "So why is it that you write goals at work and not in your "real life?"

"Ah...I never really thought about that. Good question."

"Let me ask, why do you think the bosses at your company make you write goals?"

"That's easy, to ensure the company's success."

"So you have seen firsthand how important it is to a business' success. You have followed your leaders and helped them take control of the future. You have been a part of their success."

"Yes, when you put it that way that is correct."

"And who is the leader in your real life?"

"No one. I mean, I am I guess."

"No guess here babe, you are your only leader as I am my only leader. You are your very own chief executive officer of your life and you have a responsibility to ensure its success."

"So as my very own CEO I need to take control of my future. I need to write goals for myself. I can do that. I know how to do that. I have to think about it but it is definitely something I can do. I can lead me. I just have to figure out what it is I want to achieve at this point in my life and going forward. I guess I was thinking that at my age, my goals were behind me. I know, I know you wouldn't agree with that, I am sure. After I hear it coming out of my mouth, I don't agree with me either."

"Ha ha, babe."

And on that note, lunch is served. "Perfect timing," Lucille declares.

Perfect nothing! There it is, right in front of me—my lunch—a mound of raw meat with a one-eyed raw egg sitting on top looking straight at me! I stare right back at it and pray it is dead enough not to move. Lucille distracts me by squeezing her bib into my half-closed fist.

When I fully open my hand, I am taken aback. Given that everything she is wearing is black and white, and that each day her bib is the same color as her outfit, I am surprised to see a metallic gray vinyl bib resting in my palm.

Lucille notices my jaw drop and quickly interjects with a smirk, "You were expecting a black or white bib, I presume? You know, not everything is always black or white."

"Yes, Lucille, there are many shades of gray."

"Babe, you know sometimes your game plan gets thrown a curve ball. Watch for it. Plan for it."

I got the message. And I assure her, I will be on the alert.

I look again at my lunch and am thrilled to see it comes with a potato. I taste the steak tartare and it really isn't that bad. I just have a hard time reconciling whatever it is I am eating. I congratulate myself for sampling the meat and as a reward devour my sour cream laden baked potato.

"Babe, whatever happened to "Vinnie"? Did you ever see him again?"

That inquiry seemed to come from left field but knowing Lucille files everything I say in compartmentalized folders, I figured sooner or later she would ask for an update. I hear myself laugh out loud first at the question and then at the thought of "Vinnie."

Lucille hears my laugh. "What's so funny?" which translates to "Tell me. Tell me."

I hold back my amusement to tell about a chance meeting with "Vinnie" at a corporate function when I was already married and my daughter was a few years old.

"So how was Mr. Barbarino? Did your heart flutter?"

"Well, Lucille, sorry to say, when I finally ran into my fantasy man my heart did not skip one single beat. I was living in the real world by that time. And "Vinnie" only bore a vague resemblance to the svelte and suave dreamboat of years before. His bushy head of brown hair was replaced by a shiny scalp. His bulbous belly hung over his belt a few inches. I swear he was wearing the same double-breasted, gabardine, olive green, three piece suit with cream colored shirt and maroon striped power tie. Only now, the suit was ill fitting and iridescent from wear, the shirt was more beige and the tie was faded and powerless."

"A case in point why you should periodically revisit your goals. Ha, ha, ha, ha, ha!" Lucille enjoys my exaggerated commentary and we share a hearty laugh.

Lucille takes a few small bites of the tartar and resumes the conversation. With the same frankness I have come to expect from her, she reveals her very private goals. She makes known that whenever she revisits the goals she made earlier in her life, she feels a personal satisfaction with her accomplishments. She packs her successes in her personal portfolio which she carries with her every single day of her life no matter where she goes. You could say she is tied to her success portfolio.

She discloses that her primary goal was to ensure her children's success. And the goal was realized when each of her three children finished school with one becoming a lawyer, one a doctor, and another a business woman. This was her crowning achievement. And she wears the crown proudly and without excuses. As for herself, she admits that one of her goals was to make sure that she had enough money to live comfortably as she got older. Belonging to the country club was a part of that plan.

One would have to be an idiot not to be impressed by her many successes. However I am focused on the second goal she shared with me because it was strictly about her—to live comfortably as she grew older. I have to admit that I initially rushed to judgment about her financial status. I thought that her wealth was bestowed, inherited, or married into. Now I know she earned it. Every penny of it. She never ceases to amaze me.

She tells me, "When my husband and I moved to this small town, we bought a big house. It had huge front and back porches. And a nice sized lot right in the city. My husband had his medical office in the basement. There were four floors to this house. It had about twenty rooms. All the rooms were quite large. It was a grand place and it had lots and lots of closet space. I loved it there. I was so proud. After all, it was my home. I truly imagined I would live there until I wasn't living any more. At least that was my plan."

While she is describing her house, my mind pictures a majestic-looking, old Victorian style grand structure which due to the era in which it was built lacked proper insulation and modernization. "Wow, Lucille, that must have been expensive to heat and upkeep."

"You are sharp as a tack, babe. But I have to admit, at the time, I was not too quick to realize how my goal to live in the big house would keep me from achieving my other goal of financial independence. So that is why I raised smart kids! When we sat down to discuss the situation, I realized that I had to make a major change—I could not achieve both of my goals—to live in my big home and be financially secure."

"So, I bet you sold the big house, moved into a smaller home, took the equity from the big house, and invested wisely."

"Babe, you are a genius! That is exactly what I did."

"And you know what else you did, Lucille?"

"Refresh my memory babe," she says as if conceding me her time.

"You changed your perspective, let go of the past, and took control of the future. Am I right?"

As I summarize I feel like a Jedi speaking with Yoda, my Jedi Master.

In true Lucille style, she smiles, nods, winks and raises her glass of Jack Daniel's to toast me, "Salute, babe! That is how I am able to be here today with you, with everyone!"

Lucille takes a big gulp. I suck up the final ounce of iced tea through my straw.

"You know babe, taking control of my future took me where I wanted to go. And taking control of your future will take you where you want to go. We each have different priorities and goals that we need to sort through. We are uniquely different, just like no two diamonds are the same."

Whenever Lucille speaks about diamonds, her face lights up. She has the beauty and natural allure of a well polished gemstone. Anyone can see she is as distinctive as the diamonds themselves. I find her enchanting.

Lucille seems to be enjoying her tartar. I pick at my meat without much interest. I am, however, quite pleased with myself for trying the delicacy and swear I will never venture there again unless, of course, Lucille asks me to.

Our server is monitoring our progress from across the room. She swoops in just as we place our forks and knives across our plates to signal we are done. As she removes our plates, Lucille preempts her recital of the dessert menu and lets her know that neither one of us will be having anything else to eat. It is getting late.

We talked a lot this lunch hour and the range of emotions has left both of us exhausted. Nevertheless, as I prepare to bid Lucile adieu, the procession of admirers begins. Men and women of all shapes and sizes make the pilgrimage to our table and Lucille, almost miraculously, is reenergized. Somehow, some way, Lucille musters megatons of energy to great each person warmly. Along with each kiss and hug, not surprisingly, a pleasant comment for Lucille's creative headwear is offered. I hear, "You look so cute." "Only you could wear that hat." "You never cease to amaze me." I reflect on the compliments. I agree, I agree, and I agree.

The clock is ticking and I must leave. I rise from my chair, hug and kiss Lucille, and check to see if we are on for lunch tomorrow. "You bet, babe. Looking forward to seeing you again."

"See you tomorrow, Lucille."

Walking out of the dining room always evokes a range of feelings for me as I sense the members staring at me. Sometimes I even think I hear them whisper, "She is just a guest, I have never seen her before. Does she belong here?"

Today, I am sure the asides are, "Ah...she had lunch with Lucille, she must be a special woman." I glance back at Lucille just as I am about to exit her sight range and notice two young gentleman and three young women have pulled up chairs around her at the table. My guess is they are her grandchildren. I am confident they know their good fortune.

I feel a sense of urgency as I get into my car. I need to return to the office to finish up a few things as I am scheduled for an evening rendezvous with my daughter. For the first time in a very long time I am actually looking forward to being with her. Like many mothers and daughters we have a lot of history, some good, some not so good. Regardless, my daughter looks to me and I need to lead by example, to be that model, maybe to even be her Lucille.

The drive back to the office is a challenge. It is raining "cats and dogs" as the expression goes. I call my daughter to see if she wants to come over to the house when the rain slows, instead of going out for dinner. She is fine with the change of plans. She suggests we have take-out and asks for my order.

I have a quick and easy response, "Bring anything but steak tartar."

Later in the evening, when my daughter arrives, I instinctively greet her at the door with a, "Good to see you, sweetheart." I hear my voice and I sound like Lucille—a tone of youthfulness, so very upbeat and welcoming.

"Hi Mom, are you OK?"

"Sure sweetheart, just fine. What's for dinner? I am hungry."

We haphazardly set the table and dine on vegetable lo mein and egg rolls. Our girly chitchat is all over the place. Clothes, work, what happened at the dentist, what didn't happen at the grocery store, and so on and so on. Usually when we engage in small talk it is because we are trying to avoid arguing. Tonight, there is a difference. Tonight, I am actually finding enjoyment in listening to her.

As the casual conversation rolls on, we move from the straight back dining chairs in the kitchen, to the comfort of the sofa in the living room, and then to the expanse of the carpeted floor. There, lying on our backs staring at the ceiling, which my daughter is quick to correctly point out could use a coat of paint, we rather impulsively begin discussing our futures.

We share our dreams so vividly that we are able to actually "see" what we are doing, when we are doing it, whom we are with, and of course, what we are wearing. It is like watching a video with the fast forward button stuck—three years, five years, ten years, twenty years.

My daughter tells me that she would like to open a clothing boutique by the time she is twenty five. My daughter has always had a knack for sewing but this is the first time I am hearing about her entrepreneurial desires. "Mom, I hope you don't think this is stupid, but one of the most vivid dreams I have is you and me standing under the 'Grand Opening' sign together."

I ignore her hedging as there is no stupidity involved. "That sounds exciting. I bet we are laughing our heads off."

"You bet Mom. It's so fun."

"If you would like, I can help with a business plan."

"Can you really do that? That's dope! Thanks Mom."

During this time together, I feel so in control of my future. And I sense my daughter feels the same.

We talk and talk about how we will turn our dreams into our reality. Some of it is comical. Most of it is achievable. All of it is truthful.

Time passes quickly this evening and my daughter decides she needs to leave before it gets too late. Together we walk to the front door. Right before she crosses the threshold to make her way onto the porch, she puts on the breaks. She turns and looks directly into my eyes. Without saying one word she latches on to me with an intense embrace, just like she used to do when she was a small child leaving for school. When she buries her head in my chest, I can feel her heart beating in rhythm with mine. Our hug lasts one minute; one wonderful minute. When we step back from each other, I instinctively smile, nod, and wink at her. She cracks a short smile as well and whispers with a secretive voice so only I can hear, "Thank you, Mom. Thank you very much. I love you with all my heart. I will call you tomorrow and we can talk more."

I wonder what I have given my daughter this evening that she appreciates so much? Not wanting to take too long to figure it out and miss an opportunity to show my daughter I am listening, I mirror her gentle tone, "I love you too, sweetheart. I look forward to talking with you. Please drive safely. And, sweetheart, thank you, too. Thank you very much. I had fun."

As my daughter gets into her car to drive off, I realize the rain has stopped. The musty heavy humidity that lingered for so long has lifted. The air is much lighter now. I feel lighter too. It truly is an awesome night.

I load the dishwasher, press "start" and decide all my other chores can wait until the weekend. I settle into bed and turn on the TV. There on one of the movie channels is the *Wizard of Oz*. Dorothy has just begun her journey down the yellow brick road. I feel like Dorothy. I pick up a notepad and jot down my most valued priorities; some short term and some long range goals. I outline a timeline. I even include the obstacles and possible curve balls that could be thrown my way. No doubt, I will have to figure out how to hit the curve ball.

I know it is time. I have started taking control of my future. I have my own ruby slippers—only mine are made of diamonds and borrowed from Lucille, of course.

3rd DIAMOND

TAKE CONTROL OF

YOUR FUTURE

4th DIAMOND

After a relatively good night's sleep, I awake before my annoying alarm sounds. I think about Dorothy and am confident she found her way back to Kansas. I think about my daughter and am excited about where she is headed as well. I quickly review my sketchy goals, my game plan, as Lucille calls it, and smile. I firmly announce to my happy-looking image in the mirror, "I am ready to take control of my future."

When I open my clothes closet, I look right past the usual slacks and blouses. "Um...let's see...gray business suit, white blouse, black shoes and panty hose. Yeah, it's all part of it, as Lucille says."

I get in my car, glance at the clock. I am fifteen minutes ahead of schedule. I feel sharp. I feel confident. I am ready! Carpe diem, seize the day! I arrive at my office and check my calendar. My schedule is relatively uneventful. Margie arrives thirty minutes after me, gives me a catcall and asks if I have something special on my agenda as I look "cool, quite professional." Even the MBA twins offer seemingly sincere compliments. "You look totally legit." I have to admit, it feels good to be noticed.

For most of the morning, between emails and phone calls, I focus on the team project that is nearing its deadline. Each account manager has contributed her business information. Margie compiled in-depth historical data and the twins synced the electronic media. It is now up to me (since I volunteered) to coordinate the presentation. This should be easy enough and I am certain I can wrap it up in within an hour as the updated computer program, that I now know how to use, should easily tabulate the numbers, I mean matrices.

Right before I leave for lunch with Lucille I go through my ritual. I stop off in the restroom, check my outfit, and comb my hair. It's day two of exposed gray roots. The jury is still out on whether I let my hair grow out. Should I could comb it up or leave it down, wear a headband or go without a headband, cut it short or let it grow long? Obviously, no verdict yet.

Today I am ahead of schedule and arrive at the country club earlier than usual. There are few cars parked in the country club lot as lunch time traffic hasn't yet begun. As I walk into the club house, I bypass the elevator and take the stairs. Seems like a good idea at the time in spite of my high heels. I have energy and places to go and I have no reason to turn control over to a machine to take me there.

Bouncing up the staircase, the thought that Lucille might not already be in the restaurant enters my mind. A few days ago, that thought would have stopped me in my tracks and caused a one-eighty. Without Lucille, I might be "found out." This day, I have no such insecurities and make no U-turn. Even if Lucille is not there to guide me, I feel confident. I know she will arrive soon enough.

There is no need for me to wait for Lucille. When I reach the top of the stairs and enter the dining area there she is—no real surprise. She is in position at her table ready for me. She waves to me as if to get my attention through the crowd. But there is no crowd. Why is she waving at me? Is that what it feels like when someone is on the red carpet and the crowd goes wild calling out for autographs? "Yoo hoo, babe, over here! Over here!"

Whatever her motivation she is making my walk through the restaurant fun. And fun is exactly what she is wearing. From head to toe, yellow, yellow,

yellow! She is draped in sunshine. She beams with a broader than usual grin to lead me to my seat. I am basking in her warm, radiant glow.

Blouse, slacks, scarf, pocketbook, shoes, and of course jewelry—all yellow. Her blouse has very fine pleats that expand a bit further than they probably should around her breasts. Nonetheless, it goes perfectly with her cropped pants and whimsically tied scarf. A closer look reveals smiley faces etched into her large, circular, button earrings. The rest of her jewelry, strands of neck beads and bracelets, seem to smile even without the etching.

Wait! There is a difference! There is a major difference! Lucille's beautiful white wavy hair is not hidden under a hat. Lucille is not wearing a hat. Yes, it's true, Lucille is not wearing a hat! Instead she is sporting a yellow visor! As I get closer to her I can see there is an image atop the stiff bill. The logo is a replica of the four-diamond brooch that rests upon her heart and is pinned ever so gently to her blouse so as not to upset the natural accordion folds of the fabric. Is this woman for real? A ninety-two year old camera-friendly model just waiting for her close-up!

I strut with pride in my pantyhose and business attire knowing she is watching and rooting for me. Big hug, big kiss—big hello, to my good friend, Lucille!

Lucille reciprocates with a bigger, "Hi ya babe, so very good to see you."

Always fascinated by Lucille's apparel, I usually extend an initial comment as soon as I sit down. Today, Lucille is quick as a flash and turns the introductory comment to my outfit.

"Babe, you're wearing your power attire. How attractive you look. It is such a pleasure to see you dressed so nicely. You look brilliant."

"Awesome?"

"You're funny, babe—OK awesome. You have a skip in your step, just like Dorothy on the Yellow Brick Road."

Is she kidding me? Did she make a reference to the *Wizard of Oz* movie I was watching last night? That is eerie.

"Now you are the one being funny Lucille. Or should I call you my good witch, Glinda?"

We laugh together; each probably for separate reasons.

I take a few minutes to bring Lucille up to date about my daughter and our visit the previous evening. And then I tell her about how I am taking control of my future and how I am writing down a few goals and what I need to have in place in order to achieve them.

Lucille asks, "So how does your new look fit in?"

There are two ways to answer that question. I could give a rather lengthy explanation about my work environment and my desire not to be "Mrs. Kirklandized" or I could let it go and offer Lucille the abridged version. I choose the latter. The rest is not important at this time in my life.

"Well, Lucille, several years ago I was passed over for a promotion at work."

"Why do you think they passed you over?"

Keeping with my decision to stick to the short version, I answer, "For whatever reason my boss may have had, I now know the real reason."

"And the real reason is?" Lucille asks with the same voice inflection of a celebrity presenter opening the winning envelope at the Oscars.

"Simple, it was not my time. I wasn't ready."

"And now?"

"It's time. I am ready, willing, and going to achieve it! And as you say, the look is all part of it."

"So if I hear you correctly, now you know that before you can be anything or do anything, you first need to know who you are and where you want to go."

"Yes, Lucille. I realize that now. And it has taken me this long for it to dawn on me and for me to act on it. Ah, those crystals are coming in handy."

We smile at each other. Lucille readjusts herself in her chair to sit more erect. "I love your upbeat attitude. I am energized by your enthusiasm and I am sure others will be as well."

Lucille's feedback about my attitude is rewarding.

"Lucille, you always have such a positive attitude."

"How do you know that?"

"For one, you are always smiling. You say nice things to people to make them feel good about themselves and comfortable around you. You are direct yet kind with the way you speak. You have a sense of humor and you are always willing to laugh at yourself. People are drawn to you. And you..."

Surprisingly, Lucille appears uncharacteristically uncomfortable with the accolades and taps my hand as if to signal me to shut-up. "Hey, is this a roast or something?"

"C'mon, just look at you Lucille in all your yellow, I love it, you are all about fun!"

"OK, OK, I see you get me. LOL"

What? Did she just add a LOL, laugh out loud tag? I have to know, "LOL?"

"Yes, LOL, Life of Lucille."

This is definitely a time to laugh out loud—and we both do. Again, each probably for our separate reasons.

Our waitress comes to the table and inquires, "What's going on here? You two are having too much fun!"

Indeed we are, indeed we are.

Then, with Lucille and the waitress as my audience, I make an official announcement. "I am happy to say that this afternoon I do not have to go back to my office. I am all caught up with my work and I am taking a personal half-day. So, I will have a cocktail. Will you join me Lucille?"

The two of them offer quiet applause and without skipping a beat, Lucille commands, "Two glasses of champagne!"

Shaking her head in amusing disbelief, our waitress leaves our table and walks directly to the bar.

Lucille happily gushes, "I am glad you are joining me for a cocktail today. It's a holiday."

Boy oh boy, this woman can find any reason to celebrate. What a glorious outlook!

"Lucille I have to ask, have you always had such a positive attitude?"

Lucille jumped right on the answer to my question as if she anticipated me asking, "You know babe, it's a choice. Attitude is a choice. You know that."

"Yes, I see it on billboards, hear it on talk shows, and I read about it in self-help books."

"And still some people have a hard time with it," she adds almost surprised by her observation.

"Babe, about ten years ago, I had a heart attack."

"Don't give me that you were happy to have a heart attack?"

"Ha, babe, not even I could spin that. Although I am happy to have lived through it," she quips, seeming quite pleased with herself for such a quick comeback.

The bartender makes an unprecedented fast turnaround of our drink order. Our champagne arrives almost instantaneously, as if Lucille just snapped her fingers and two elegant fluted stemmed glasses filled with sparkling wine appear from nowhere. Presto! How celebratory! Lucille is magical!

Without hesitation and in perfect unison, we lift the bubbly, "Salute, Cent'anni!" With the precision of synchronized swimmers, we clink our glasses, smile, nod, and wink at each other as we take our first sip.

"AH..." Lucille proclaims.

"AH..." I parrot.

It is a toss-up as to who is savoring the moment more, me or Lucille.

After our first refreshing sip, Lucille continues, "So I had this heart attack. No history of heart problems, ever. They rush me in an ambulance and to the intensive care unit at the hospital. My sons are there watching over me like hawks. But the first person I see when I wake up is my daughter. To be honest, I was not too happy to see her."

"Wait a minute, I am confused. Why would you not be happy to see your daughter? Were you fighting with her or something?"

"Oh no, nothing like that. My daughter and her husband, I never told you about my son-in-law—he is such a good boy—but sometimes I think they take life a bit too seriously. So when I saw her sitting next to my bed, I asked her what she was doing there. I asked her, aren't you supposed to be on vacation, why are you here?"

Lucille pauses just long enough for another taste of champagne.

"My daughter snapped at me, 'Mom you had a heart attack; I thought I should be here.' "

Personally, I thought her daughter responded appropriately. Lucille, on the other hand, is not always predictable so I give her a lead-in and say, "To which you replied…"

"Never let anyone get in your way of having fun."

Slowly, I repeat the phrase. "Never let anyone get in your way of having fun. Catchy sentiment, Lucille. But don't you think your daughter should have been at your beside?"

"Perhaps, and especially if my sons were not there. But my sons were there and there was absolutely nothing she could do other than watch me sleep. And on top of that I would have felt a lot better if she would lighten up, go on vacation, and enjoy life a bit more. So I seized an opportunity to remind her."

"I'd say you did. I am sure she got the message."

"Loud and clear, babe! She reminds me about it all the time now," she says laughingly. "You know I sometimes wonder who raised her," and once again Lucille laughs at her own joke.

Cute Lucille, very cute. "I guess you never let a good teaching opportunity get away."

"Absolutely, never. It's my job."

I guess I should have known she would say that. She has this sense of commitment to share with others what she has learned and what she has done purely for their benefit.

We both raise our glasses of the bubbly and again imbibe.

"Babe, do you know the song *You've Got to Accentuate the Positive, Eliminate the Negative?* she asks while singing the first couple of bars.

A few days ago, I was embarrassed for both of us when she broke into song. Today, I join the chorus, "Don't mess with Mr. In-between."

"Well I sing it a lot. Looking at situations or people in a positive way is a choice; a choice I make each day. And it makes me feel good. It reduces my stress."

"Is that why your skin doesn't show all those worry lines?"

"It could be. It's all part of it. You know attitude shows up all over—in your face, in your health, in what you wear, in how you treat people, how people treat you; in so many different ways. And the great thing about attitude is that you have total control over it. Only you get to make the choice about your own attitude."

She pauses for one short moment and proclaims, "Now that is truly awesome!"

Our waitress strolls by our table to inquire, "Ladies, are you going to eat sometime today?"

The dining room is almost entirely filled by this time so we are both figuring it is time to order. "But of course, darling," responds Lucille in her best Hollywood siren voice. Neither one of us refers to our menus or gives our server time to recite the scheduled specials. Lucille simply inquires, "Do you think the chef can make me an open-faced tuna melt with a slice of tomato on pumpernickel bread?" I follow Lucille's lead and go rogue as well, "And may I have a bowl of chili?"

For the first time since we have been having lunch together, we order different entrees. Maybe it was the champagne, maybe not.

"Babe, have you ever been in a beauty pageant?"

Before I can even answer her with an "absolutely no way" she says, "I was in a beauty pageant. I was old enough to collect social security at the time."

What in the world is she talking about?

"There were about a dozen of us senior women from all over the county. One woman was a concert pianist, another sang like an opera diva, and one even danced. It was something; the first of its kind in the area."

I know she wants me to ask, so I do, "What was your talent?"

"I belted out the song *New York, New York*. I wore a three-piece, pin-striped tuxedo, with a top hat and cane and sang my heart out."

"It must have been fun."

"I wouldn't have done it if it wasn't fun. You know that."

Yes, I know that. "So how did it go?"

"Half way through my song, my hat fell off. I couldn't bend over to get it so you know what I did?"

I can't wait to hear how she handled the snafu. "What did you do?"

"I kept singing and smiling and I took my cane and flipped up my hat with my cane."

"Oh my goodness! Did the crowd go wild?"

"They sure did."

"Did you know you would be able to do that? Had you practiced?"

"It was pure luck."

"It must have been quite a sight! I can see you strutting back and forth on the apron of the stage singing 'Start spreading the news,' with your cane on your shoulder and your hat falls off and you twirl your cane down and catch the tip under the brim and flip it up—like something right out of vaudeville."

"My goodness babe, were you there?"

"I was not, Lucille. Although I wish I had been. I would have loved to have seen your face when they handed you your trophy."

"How did you know I won?"

"Lucille, you're attitude makes you stand out from other women. Your confident, sophisticated attitude is what draws people to you. It's what makes you so attractive. It's what makes you a winner—someone so aware of her finest asset. Do you really think the other women had a chance?"

"Is the roast continuing?"

"I apologize if I make you uncomfortable. I'm learning so much from you. I guess it is my way of saying thank you for all you are doing for me."

"You have done for me as well, babe," Lucille says tenderly as she taps my hand.

And on that quiet note, our meals are served.

Our conversation during our lunch, as all the days previous, meanders in one direction and then another direction, just like typical women. We learn a little more about each other—our likes and dislikes, favorite movies and television shows, who has what on sale, and where to shop for shoes.

Lucille tells me more about her "boys," as she calls her sons, and how hard they worked to get where they are today and how truly proud she is of both of them. She tells me more about her daughter and how the older she gets the closer they get. She also notes that her daughter owns a company and is an author.

I am thinking her daughter should write a book about her but I don't dare say anything as I do not want to interrupt her train of thought.

Lucille continues telling me more about her loved ones including her grandchildren and great grandchildren. She reaches into her purse and pulls out a four by six inch family photo. She is obviously very proud.

She then asks if I want to see a picture of her pride and joy.

"Sure," as I anticipate seeing her dog or some other pet.

Instead she whips out a crinkled, apparently well-traveled photo of furniture polish and dish detergent—Pride and Joy. I shake my head in disbelief while my fun-loving friend smirks, obviously self-satisfied she put one over on me.

Lucille strategically replaces the pictures back into a small compartment in her purse. I get the feeling she wants to ensure she has complete and easy access to them when she pulls the caper on another unsuspecting companion.

After the photos are safe and secure, she continues to tell me about her daughter-in-law and son-in-law. Her daughter-in-law has recently been appointed "#1 designated driver." Lucille dubbed her such a title as she does all the taxiing now that she no longer drives herself.

I can hear the gratefulness in her voice, "My daughter-in-law has become my chauffer. Her mother and I are like sisters. We go around together. My daughter-in-law drives the both of us wherever we need to go."

When it comes time to speak about her son-in-law, she just shakes her head and gives a motherly expression of approval, "He is such a good boy. It's no wonder, he comes from good stock. His father was a loving and beloved man. And his mother, who is my age, has a computer, and even more than that, she knows how to use it. How 'bout that!"

Lucille is obviously excited for her son-in-law's mother's skill, a skill she herself does not possess. And then she proclaims, "My son-in-law nicknamed me 'the eternal teenager.' He's funny. He is such a good boy."

I am sure he is, Lucille.

It is comforting, and not one bit shocking, to learn that Lucille has a loving and supportive family. Many years ago, she made them her priority and now she is reaping the benefits.

As Lucille talks, I eat. I finish my chili. The portion size is just enough. Lucille doesn't finish her tuna melt. The portion is not that large. Perhaps she was talking too much or really wasn't that hungry as she explained to justify the leftovers. I did think it was odd and unlike her to leave so much food on her plate, but I said nothing.

Our waitress removes our dishes. Lucille reminds her, "Put the sandwich in a doggie bag please and bring me a cappuccino."

"I will have a cappuccino as well."

"This is really a party," she adds apparently pleased that I am able to have coffee with her.

A short time later the waitress serves our frothed coffee. "Perfect," we both agree. Within a second after our first slurp, someone comes up from behind us. Like all the other visitors to the table, this visitor hugs and kisses Lucille. And then, much to my surprise I, too, feel a hug and gentle peck on my cheek. As I look back to see who it is, the four-diamond brooch gives her away. It's Kitty!

"Kitty, I am so glad to see you."

Lucille waves to get our server's attention. "Kitty, you want coffee, dessert, something to eat? How about three quarters of an open-faced grilled tuna melt with a slice of tomato on pumpernickel bread?"

"Always looking out for me aren't you. I just had lunch with Bob. I would like a cup of coffee. I am watching my girlish figure these days, Lucille."

"I am watching it too, Kitty. You are so very attractive, you know that," Lucille says with a motherly tone.

"I agree."

"Why thank you both. So what have the two of you been doing these days?" Kitty inquires as if she didn't already know the answer.

"Kitty, I have had lunch with Lucille for the past four days. And I think it would take me four weeks to tell you all about it."

"Sounds like quite an eventful time." Kitty correctly surmises.

"Kitty, I am so very grateful that you introduced me to Lucille. I am following her lead and am on a quest to make my age my best asset."

"How are you doing that?"

"Let me give you a summary. First, I am changing my perspective. Second, I am letting go of the past. And third, I am taking control of my future."

"Is there a fourth?"

"Oh my, how could I forget? It's all about attitude"

Lucille seems truly pleased with 'Grasshopper.' I catch the cohorts sneaking a shared wink, obviously satisfied with my accomplishments and new-found knowledge.

"I am so grateful to both you and Lucille," I gush.

Kitty picks up on my thought. "You know each night when I go to bed, I write down all the things for which I am grateful. Sometimes I have as many as fifty items on my list. Things like a parking space with time on the meter, or a beautiful sunny day, or a rainy day, a phone call from my grandchildren, an unscheduled lunch with my husband, a smile from the cashier at the supermarket...you get the idea. With those comforting thoughts, my mind is at peace and I easily fall asleep. And you know that a good night's rest is vital for a sharp mind and good skin."

Lucille agrees with Kitty, "How true."

"Lucille do you do that, too?"

"Having a gratitude attitude, keeps you on the positive side," Lucille adds.

"That makes sense. And then you wake up feeling that way," I chime in.

"Yes. What Lucille taught me was to wake up with a song in my heart. Sing a tune and set the tone is how she put it. Right, Lucille?"

Lucille commends Kitty for her sharp memory.

"Really, you didn't tell me that Lucille."

"That's why Kitty is here, she is going to give us a rendition of her morning song."

"Very funny, Lucille. You are the singer in the group. You are the one who visits hospitals and nursing homes to sing to sick and less fortunate people. What's your song?"

Lucille seems to be waiting to be asked. "I have a few. I have to change up every now and then to spread the wealth. This week my song is *On the Sunny Side of the Street.*"

And with that we all sing, Lucille with the loudest voice of course, "Grab your coat, and get your hat, leave your worries on the doorstep, life can be so sweet on the sunny side of the street." Quite surprisingly, the other diners join in and sing along. When we finish all the verses, the impromptu choir claps and hoots. It is like something out of a movie. Everyone in the dining area, members, guests, and wait staff are all laughing and applauding. It is such fun. And all the fun orchestrated by Lucille. What a celebration!

I turn to Kitty, "So my friend what is your song?"

"OK, I will tell you but I will skip the singing. For the last few weeks it has been Carol King's *Beautiful.*"

"You've got to get up every morning with a smile on your face. And show the world all the love in your heart," I chime in as a solo vocalist.

"Yup, that's the one."

"OK, I will have to come up with my morning song to start my day. I will let you know tomorrow. Tonight I am going to work on my gratitude list. I already know two names I will include on it. You are both such gems."

Lucille glances Kitty's way and in unison they question, "Diamonds?"

"But of course darlings, you know diamonds are a girl's best friend," doing a poor impersonation of Lucille as the country club siren.

Kitty and Lucille are amused. And with that, I bid them both good-bye.

I rise from my chair and walk over to Kitty and extend a quick hug and kiss. I then walk around to Lucille and do the same, just as I have done every day for the entire week.

She reminds me we are on for lunch again tomorrow. Already I cannot wait. I signal my delight with a thumbs-up gesture.

Exiting the country club is a breeze.

4ᵗʰ DIAMOND

CHOOSE A GRATITUDE ATTITUDE

Annarose Ingarra-Milch

THE SILVER CHAIN

Before I went to bed last night, I replayed my lunch with Lucille. I remembered Lucille and Kitty encouraging me to jot down those things for which I am thankful. Of course, Lucille's friendship and her trusted sidekick, Kitty, were right at the top of the list, along with my relationship with my daughter, my awesome health, and opportunity at work. I really thought it was going to be a daunting task but it was a peaceful and stress releasing experience and it led me to one of my best night's sleep—EVER!

I wake up with the Rascals song *A Beautiful Morning* playing in my head. "It's a beautiful morning. I think I'll go outside for a while and just smile." As I am singing, I am also smiling which is something I rarely do at this time of day. The tune is actually setting the tone, just like Lucille and Kitty said it would.

Today is my fifth lunch with Lucille and I can't wait to get to the country club to see her. I have so much to tell her. I am actually feeling good about myself. I look in the mirror and see a different woman. This woman is more confident, smarter, and even quite attractive.

My morning hours in the office are routine. Talk of another change in the corporate structure is in the air and supposedly the staff from one of the branch offices will be moving in with us at this site. People are already complaining about their cramped quarters. The strange thing is that today I am simply appreciative that I have a job and any work space at all. It resembles the feeling I had when I was housed in my multi-use, second floor, storage closet. There is an email blast notifying everyone that another interior renovation to make room for growth will begin in the upcoming weeks. Man, I am way ahead of them.

Although I am on time for lunch with Lucille, the county club parking lot is full. My usual spot by the pro shop is already occupied which requires me to circle around the back of the clubhouse, past the designated handicapped parking area and into the overflow section. This makes my walk to the clubhouse a bit longer than usual but gives me opportunity to exercise. When I enter the building, I compound my physical activity by ignoring the elevator, as I did yesterday, to take full advantage of the stairs. I know Lucille will already be at her table and I can't wait to be with her.

I pause at the top of the staircase to catch my breath and then begin my walk into the dining area. Lo and behold! Lucille is a "golden girl." From the top of her gold-sequin beret to the bottom of her gold, rhinestone studded shoes, she is draped in gold. Her long-sleeve gold lame dress is simple yet gracefully stylish and fits her well. And although it has its own decorative collar, Lucille raises the elegance factor a notch with a flowing gold rope necklace and matching hoop earrings. She shines as brightly as the exit sign in a dark theatre and my eyes fix on her.

The outfit is stunning. The jewelry is stunning. And the four-diamond brooch she wears over her heart is stunning. Lucille is royalty.

Perhaps because it is unusually crowded or maybe because she misjudged my arrival time, Lucille is not looking in my direction when I enter the restaurant. I catch her fidgeting in her seat as if she is uncomfortable. She appears to be sitting low. And then, as if the director yells "action," she shifts her body ever so slightly to improve her posture and the model is once again on set and ready for the photographers.

There is no other way to describe her other than to say she looks like a queen. She exudes a purposeful presence from her dining room throne and even though her court is quite full, she sends me a personal message with her regal smile that she is "ready" to see me. I advance directly toward her, honored to be summoned.

I step to the table. "Hi ya babe," Lucille greets me. I hug and kiss her. She pats me on the arm as we embrace and simultaneously say, "Good to see ya!"

I have so much to tell Lucille today. I want to tell her all about what is going on at work, at home—in my life. I want to tell her that I have started to look at my age from a different perspective and realize that I am smart and I have valuable skills to offer. I want to tell her that it is actually getting easier to let go of the past and all the baggage that weighs me down and makes it impossible for me to grab a hold of opportunity and move forward. I want to let her know that I am taking control of my future and setting realistic goals for myself. I want to tell her that I have changed my attitude about the value of my age, about me as a person, about what I am supposed to be doing at this time in my life and that I am so very grateful for all I have and all I am able to do. I want to tell her what a life changing experience it has been to watch her, listen to her, and learn from her. I even want to sing her my morning tune that set the tone for my day. I want to tell her so much.

As my mind is racing, I notice the waitress standing next to Lucille. Usually she allows us time to chit chat before she visits our table. This time, instead of asking for our drink order or telling us about the specials, she places her hand on Lucille's shoulder, bends over and whispers in Lucille's ear, "Are you feeling alright?"

Oh my goodness! In my haste to share all the good news about me, I fail to notice that although all the golden props are in place Lucille's beautiful skin looks ashen and her voice is weak. She places her hand on mine, "Babe, you don't mind if we skip lunch today. Could you drive me home?"

"I would be happy to do whatever you want me to do, Lucille."

As Lucille gingerly rises from her chair, leaning heavily on the table for leverage, she instructs me to retrieve her handicapped walker that is tucked in the corner of the room out of her reach and up until today, out of my sight.

Once she is upright and her hands are secured on the walker, we begin our exit from the dining room. Lucille stands as tall as a woman of five feet is possibly able. She leads the way. I follow behind her. Our procession moves ever so slowly. She roles her four-wheeled walker past the first and the second and the third table and every table. She moves her head right, takes a few steps and moves her head left. She makes eye contact and extends a royal nod to as many of her subjects as she possibly can. And each one she passes respectfully delays their next bite of food to acknowledge her presence and her passing. There is an air of quiet reverence in the room. Several members of her court reach out to touch her. "Good bye, Lucille." "Be well, Lucille." "See you tomorrow, Lucille." She responds with a gracious nod and kind smile.

Right before I direct her to the elevator in the lobby, Lucille tenderly touches my arm to redirect me.

"We'll need to take the other elevator to go thru the basement. That is where the ramp is."

Lucille never told me that she has to walk through the lowest level to get to the dining area. My image of this strong woman was that she made her entrance like a movie star on the red carpet gliding through the country club hallways glad-handing everyone, like all the other members.

Taking the service elevator, we make our way into the bowels of the beautiful club house. We walk past the smelly bins of dirty table linens and exit through the back service door which leads to the handicapped ramp. Luckily I am parked close to the rear of the building. When we are finally secure in my car, Lucille fumbles through her purse for her gold leather sunglass case and puts on her Audrey Hepburn fashionista sunglasses. It is not a very sunny day and I am curious as to why she needs to wear them. I don't ask.

As we drive out of the country club parking lot and down the long, winding driveway, Lucille provides directions to her home. After that, the ride is a quiet one. Every once in a while I say something just to pass the time and distract her. She rarely responds. Her silence is telling. She does not feel well. When I ask how she is feeling, she offers a vague answer, "I am just tired. Could use a little rest. That's all." And of course, she says it with a smile, probably so I do not worry about her.

We arrive at her home and pull into the driveway. I remove her walker from the trunk of the car. She struggles to hoist herself out of the car and I offer a forceful tug. Then she walks five steps to the front stairs. At the stoop, she abandons the walker and pulls herself up the three wooden stairs using the handrail for leverage. I put the walker in front of her at the top of the stairs for her to grab hold. She hands me her set of keys which are on an orange, rubber, scrunchy, wristband keychain with a dangling red stiletto high heel charm and I unlock the door. The keychain is so Lucille!

The door opens directly into the kitchen. It is a small ranch-style home perfectly designed for Lucille. With a relatively open floor plan, I can see Lucille's personal touches everywhere. The kitchen counter tops are mauve colored as is the kitchen tile floor. The living room carpet is a coordinating pink which complements the white, pink and gray floral furniture.

There is an easy blend of new furniture and vintage pieces. She obviously had taken from her big house and times gone by and simply blended those items of importance into her newer home.

One specific wall hanging catches my eye. I walk up to it as Lucille is putting her purse on the door knob of the hallway closet. It is a quote accredited to Ralph Waldo Emerson entitled *"Persistence."* My curiosity with Emerson's work does not go unnoticed by Lucille.

"Babe, read the quote. Read it to me slowly."

I follow her directive and read loudly and slowly so we both can absorb the message.

"That which we persist in doing becomes easier.

Not that the nature of the task has changed,

But our ability to do it has increased."

Lucille, although obviously feeling ill, refuses to miss the opportunity to remind me that to really be myself I will have to constantly work at it and work on it. It will take persistence.

Then she asks, "Babe, do you remember when you were learning to ride a two wheel bike?"

"Sure do, Lucille."

"And what happened as you were learning?"

"I kept falling off. I still have a scar on my leg from one of the falls."

"And then what happened?"

"I got back on the bike."

"Yes, babe, it was your persistence, even with scraps and scratches that enabled you to master the bike. The bike never changed. But you did."

"You know Lucille I bet I could ride a bike today if I had the opportunity."

"I am confident you could. Now, as you go forward, you may fall again because life can be difficult. There are challenges and setbacks. You know that. You have lived through them. You have learned from them. And you always came out of them better than before. So, please never give up."

"I hear you, Lucille. I hear you." I don't want her to speak anymore because her voice is growing weaker with each word. I know she needs to lie down. I help her unclasp her jewelry and take off her hat and shoes. Before she goes into her bedroom to lie down and rest, she turns to remind me, "Remember, you are your best asset—at any age."

She smiles and winks at me.

"I love you, Lucille."

"I love you too, babe".

Holding tightly to her deeply affectionate words, I leave.

I return to the office feeling somewhat unsettled. Margie pops her head around the partition and asks about my lunch with Lucille. I don't want to explain so I respond, "It went OK". Then she confides, "I had a hard time coming to work today. I bet no one would have noticed if I didn't show up at all."

"Margie. Let's have lunch. Real soon. My treat."

After Margie withdraws behind the iron curtain, Ms. MBA stops by my desk to inquire about my lunch with Lucille. Again, I avoid a lengthy explanation and reiterate what I told Margie, "It went OK."

Ms. MBA moves closer to me, seemingly trying to mustering up her nerve, and asks if we (as in she and I) could meet for lunch some day so she can pick my brain about how I would handle a situation she is struggling with.

"Sure, I would like that. Whenever you are ready, let me know."

As she steps away she turns to offer departing remarks, "You know you look good with gray hair. I can't wait until I have some gray hair to show off."

When I hear the words coming from my colleagues and I think about all that has gone on in my life these past few days, I feel Lucille everywhere. I now realize what "being me" actually means. At this point in my life it is time to lead. It is time to be a model, like Lucille, a role model. It is time to show through my words and actions that my age is my best asset.

The rest of the afternoon at work drags and I am ready and most thankful the weekend is here. On Saturday and Sunday, I do my usual household chores. In fact, I bury myself in my chores so I do not worry about Lucille. I clean closets, scrub floors, and even repaint the living room ceiling. My sleep is restless. I want to call Lucille but I don't want to bother her. I miss her more than I would ever have imagined. I need my "Lucille fix."

The several texts and phone calls I place to Kitty go unanswered until Monday morning. Early Monday, before I leave for work, I receive a text-message followed by a phone call, "Hey, it's Kitty. Meet me at Lucille's."

I hold back my excitement, "For lunch? At her table at the country club?"

"No, at her home." Kitty's words make me want to throw up. My entire body senses something is not right.

When I arrive at Lucille's house, there are two cars in the driveway. Kitty's is one of them. The other one I don't recognize because it has out-of-state license plates.

I walk up the front stairs and tap on the door. The door is ajar and opens slowly without much effort. There standing in the kitchen is Kitty with another woman. The other woman is about my age. She has beautiful silver hair and wears a sad smile. And although she is conservatively dressed, almost an exact opposite of Lucille, I recognize her to be Lucille's daughter. I walk straight to her and hug her as if I had known her all my life. She embraces me with the same heartfelt intensity. We exchange no words. None are necessary.

When we unlock our bodies from each other, Lucille's daughter explains that Lucille passed away last evening. Her announcement takes my breath away and I am weak in the knees. She guides me to the safety of a kitchen chair to regain my composure.

As I sit, I listen to her explain that in her daily phone calls with her mom, Lucille told her about her last week and an "awesome" woman she had the pleasure to have lunch with at the country club.

She said this woman was so smart, so attractive, so powerful and strong. She was willing to see things from different perspectives. She was open to letting go of the past and taking control of her future. This woman understood what it meant to have an attitude filled with gratitude and positive thoughts. And on top of all of that, she was accepting that she was her best asset, at any age.

I start to cry. I can't help it. Lucille's daughter offers me a tissue. As I dry my eyes, she hands me a small silver jewelry box, clasped with a silver ribbon. There is a card attached.

I want to continue crying but I am distracted by the gift. In a quiet tone, the daughter says, "My mom asked me to give you this. She also had me write out the card to you as she could not see very well with her macular degeneration."

"What did you say? Did you say your mom could hardly see?"

That can't be, she had such vision.

"My mom had real difficulty hearing too. That is why she had two hearing aids."

No, that can't be, she listened so well.

"And of course you have seen her struggle to hold things and do things with her painful arthritic hands."

Yes, and yet she touched my heart each day with such grace.

"Not to mention her many other ailments. She had arthritis all over her body. She had two replacement hips and one replacement knee. She lived in chronic pain for almost her entire life."

I say nothing. I can't. OH MY GOODNESS! This woman had such physical limitations and at no time did she make me aware of them. If I had only one wish in my life, I would use it to ease her pain.

Kitty can see I am visibly shaken and tries to interject some humor to ease my pain, "Yup, no little old lady here!" She is partially successful as the three of us are able to force a half-hearted smile.

Once again, I look at the creative looking box with its card that Lucille's daughter had given me. I walk into the living room feeling so alone. I sit on the floral wingback chair and read the card. Although it is in her daughter's handwriting, I can hear Lucille's voice.

From the Desk of Lucille 💎 💎 💎 💎

Hi ya babe! Thank you so much for taking time out of your busy schedule to have lunch with me last week. I truly appreciate you helping me achieve one of my goals.

I wanted to eat, laugh, sing, and tip a few Jack Daniel's with someone who was bright, beautiful, and full of life.

Someone who truly understands the meaning and power behind the four Diamonds.

Someone willing to change her perspective and recognize her crystallized intelligence; someone willing to take risks and let go of the past; and someone with a game plan in place to grab control of the future. And of course someone always willing to smile at others, laugh at herself with her shortcomings, and has an attitude that sings with joy.

Someone who never lets anyone get in her way of having fun.

I wanted to spend my days with someone who knows that four Diamonds are all linked together.

Someone willing to keep the chain of persistence alive.

Someone who has learned it, done it, and through her everyday actions, looks for opportunities to teach it.

Someone well aware of where intelligence and beauty come from.

Someone who sees this time in her life as something as valuable as a precious gem.

Someone who fully realizes she is her best asset at any age--and lives accordingly.

I was blessed to have been able to spend my days with you, babe.

Take the mantel. You earned it. It is your turn.

Welcome to the club!

Lucille

Overwhelmed is the only word that can describe my emotions. I sit motionless, staring at the words on the card.

And then with true Lucille flair, I see she included a post script.

P.S. Good luck with your new awesome job!

My hands shake and my eyes fill with tears making it a slight challenge to untie the bow and open the silver box. But when I do, I can do nothing but smile. No trembling, no crying, just smiles. There within my own grasp is a four-diamond brooch, each diamond connected with a silver chain.

I can feel my grin broadening and my eyes widening, just like when I was a kid opening a present at my birthday party. Surprisingly, my hands are nimble as ever as I secure the most beautiful brooch I have ever seen in my life to the left hand side of my blouse, right over my heart.

It is not until I have completely clasped the brooch, that I look up to see that I am no longer alone. Lucille's daughter, Kitty, and thirty or forty other women—redheads, brunettes, salt and peppered, gray haired women—some with smooth, and some with deep glabellas—each one smiling at me.

We All are wearing Lucille's four-diamond brooch.

We All have been led by a woman who taught us that we are our best asset—whatever our age.

And we All with one voice cheer,

Salute Lucille, Cent'anni!

Annarose Ingarra-Milch

ABOUT THE AUTHOR

Annarose Ingarra-Milch is a professional development facilitator and celebrated national speaker.

Over the past several decades, she has drawn on her experience as an entrepreneur, corporate trainer, writer and educator to help predominately female audiences recognize and apply success principles to achieve goals, solve problems and revolutionize their careers.

Simply put, Annarose's mission has been to bring women together to learn and grow.

Her novella, *Lunch with Lucille*, is the first in a series and is intended as an inspiration to help all women realize that they are their Best Asset at any Age!

Lucille
Invites You

. . . to be part of the club!

Now you can be part of the growing group of dynamic women who have learned the important life-affirming lessons symbolized by Lucille's brooch.

And

You can proudly show it with your
VERY OWN BROOCH!

To learn more
visit us today at
www.lunchwithlucille.com